THE RACISM
OF PEOPLE WHO
LOVE YOU

THE RACISM OF PEOPLE WHO LOVE YOU

ESSAYS ON MIXED RACE BELONGING

SAMIRA K. MEHTA

BEACON PRESS
BOSTON

BEACON PRESS
Boston, Massachusetts
www.beacon.org

Beacon Press books
are published under the auspices of
the Unitarian Universalist Association of Congregations.

26 25 24 23   8 7 6 5 4 3 2 1

This book is printed on acid-free paper that meets the uncoated paper
ANSI/NISO specifications for permanence as revised in 1992.

Text design and composition by Kim Arney

Library of Congress Cataloguing-in-Publication Data is available for this title.

Hardcover ISBN: 978-08070-2636-6
E-book ISBN: 978-08070-2637-3

To Matteo
with hope for his future
and with love from his aunt.

CONTENTS

AUTHOR'S NOTE

Telling your own story is a complicated thing, in part because how you might tell a story changes over time, and in part because other people's lives are intertwined. Not only is there no way to tell one's own story without telling other people's stories—we also each remember different things and remember them through our own perspectives. I can imagine other people remembering the events that I write about differently. That is, for better or for worse, how memory works. In part because of those differences, and to protect people who might not want their stories told, I have not named the majority of my relatives. Indeed, I have seventeen aunts and uncles, and that is before you start counting my parents' cousins and close friends, all of whom (in the Indian context at least) are also aunts and uncles. Not only have I not named all of these relatives, I have sometimes conflated them—created composites, precisely to avoid telling any one person's story.

For other people, I have made a variety of choices. I have used the names of people who have given me permission to do so, like my friend Jimmy, or if they are not mentioned at length. Other times, I have simply described the relationship—this half-Asian friend, or that one; this mentor, who offered insight as someone who is also mixed; that mentor, who mentored across racial difference. In these cases, I wanted to spare the reader the need to keep track of a cast of characters, and also to preserve the anonymity of people who may have offered advice or told stories in a given moment or context, advice that mattered to me but that they might (or might not) remember and subscribe to today.

In only one case, that of my friend James, have I created a fictitious name, and once again, I am grateful to him for agreeing to have the story told.

INTRODUCTION

I started thinking about, and then writing, these essays in 2016, in the run-up to and then the aftermath of the election. I had been playing with some of the ideas for a while when, as I write in the titular essay, I went out to dinner with a very old friend. He was, as we all were, painfully aware of how much xenophobia the Trump campaign incited; whether because the campaign had created it with propaganda, or whether it simply empowered bigots to say what they were thinking, I still do not know. Indeed, by the time we had this dinner, a month or two before the election, I had twice been spit on and told to "go home" while shopping at my local grocery store, about an hour and a half outside of Philadelphia. We were discussing the question of whether I would move into the city and commute, in part to live in a place where I felt safer as a woman of color. That said, cities would prove not to feel completely safe: before the inauguration, I would be spit on while riding the metro on my way to Reagan National Airport in Washington, DC, as I flew to a conference in Rochester, New York. On that same trip, at the airport for my return flight, the Rochester TSA would go through every item in my carry-on, holding up dirty pair of panties after dirty pair of tights. Two young, nonbinary Canadians, traveling from the same conferences, would see this happening to me, and sit themselves down, with their eyes closed to protect me from embarrassment, until they knew I was safe.

My friend was horrified by the racism that I was experiencing and, as a white ally, wanted to give me space to talk about it. But as I was talking to him, I found myself trying to explain that the racism that hurts me the most is not the racism that scares me the most. It's not the racism that comes with confederate flags or that makes me fear for my safety. Rather, it's the racism of people who love me, the racism that I don't know how to see, or talk about, or name, and that because I can't quite name it as racism, it often ends up making me feel crazy.

In thinking about this kind of racism, it's important to name that I am a person of multiple heritages. My father was South Asian, as are all of his relatives, and my mother is a white midwestern American. In some ways, then, this is the story of moments when my white family and the friends that I have made through a life lived in Primarily White Institutions have been, however unintentionally, sources of racism in my life. It's hard to name these things as racism, because they are not often deliberate and because sometimes they look simply like interpersonal conflict. And that is why it is important to note that for me, even when my family doesn't realize it, often when *I* do not realize it, my ways of being in the world draw from multiple cultures and heritages. That does not mean I am always right—as my therapist could attest, I am someone who is deeply and anxiously preoccupied by the times when I have likely been wrong. It does, however, mean that racial and cultural difference come into the most intimate spaces of life.

Identifying with multiple heritages is increasingly common in the United States. According to the United States census, in 2010, 2.9 percent of the population reported multiracial heritage, while in 2020, 10.2 percent of the population did.

That percentage jump represents some 17.6 million people, an increase of more than 1,000 percent. Some 2.7 million of those people are like me, half-white and half-Asian. (It is important to note that while this number almost certainly reflects a change in the number of actual mixed race people, it also may reflect changes in how people report. While I cannot remember how I, personally, filled out my census forms, I know that I sometimes claim mixed heritage, and at other times, thinking about my name and my skin color, simply claim to be South Asian or Asian.) For a sense of proportion, the Pew Foundation estimates that American Jews make up 2.4 percent of the population, at about 5.8 million adults. I do not say this to diminish the importance of American Jews—I am, after all, a scholar of American Jewish culture. I say this more to point out that, if there are only slightly more than double the number of Jews than there are half-whites/half-Asians, our stories, important in and of themselves, are also culturally important. Even more so if there are commonalities as well as differences across mixed race experiences. Having, and claiming, multiple heritages is increasingly part of the American experience, but based on the multiple-heritaged folks that I have met through social media, it is increasingly part of the human experience.

Of course, while I am suggesting that there are (probably) commonalities across mixed experiences, and while I experience some of those commonalities while talking with friends who are Italian Mexican American, Scots Mexican, Korean Irish, Indian Cuban, Anglo-American, Chinese Irish, and Irish Iranian, there are also differences. Sometimes these differences come from how you are racialized—the history of the "one drop rule" in the United States makes it very different to be Black and something else than to be white and something else. And, of course, what those other things are matter a lot as well, as does where and how you were raised. (This range of experience can be seen in "Failing the Authenticity Test," where I contrast my experience growing up on the edges of an Indian immigrant community to those of my Korean Irish friend Jimmy, growing up on military bases where almost everyone who was Korean had a Korean mom and white, Black, or brown American dad.)

When I talk about my white family, and my white family of choice, I use the language of racism because I understand racism to be deeply tied to power. In point of fact, I experience just as much or more cultural tension in South Asian spaces as I do in white spaces. In fact, at the same time that I was thinking, with my white friend, about some moments of deep discomfort with white loved ones, I had been talking to a South Asian friend about how being someone of multiple heritages can make me feel out of step in Asian American settings, particularly settings where everyone is South Asian. In these essays, I don't tend to name that dynamic as racism, precisely because of power, but I do think about it in terms of authenticity policing. I also think some about what it means when different people of color have very different family relationships to the dominant white culture. I do not write about this experience in these essays, but I find myself thinking of when I tried to join the South Asian students' group my first year of college, and discovering that, because I am monolingual and because my white mother is the parent who did the most child-rearing, and whose culture therefore had the biggest sway in my development, that I was a problem, "white on the inside, brown on the outside." While some of that charge may have been tied to my own problematic relationship to white privilege, much of it was tied to more practical things—like having my primary comfort foods be matzo ball soup and a traditional family birthday cake as much or more than Indian dishes.

Because I am a brown woman who was primarily raised in the culture of my white mother, I am often, as my friend Tom put it as I described this book to him, culturally uncomfortable where I am racially comfortable, and racially comfortable where I am culturally uncomfortable. In some ways, that is it—certainly, there is an element of feeling very much like I am a cultural Connecticut Yankee who does not know what to do in a Hindu temple, but who also faces micro- (and sometimes) macroaggressions when within predominantly white spaces. Those are the realities that I try to tease out in the essays "Failing the Authenticity Test," "The Racism of People Who Love You," and "American Racism." But actually, at least for me, multiple identities mean a hybrid culture, which even I cannot necessarily parse, as I write about in the essay "Meat Is Murder." In that essay, I think about the multiple cultural threads that I pull together in my vegetarianism, even as I think about a desi friend who calls out high-caste people who claim that being "vegan by choice and not by religion" means that they are not casteist. Because a basic rule of structural oppression is that you do not need to know you are doing it, or even know about it to do it, I am sure I am casteist, and, as I say in my article, I also did not know that vegetarianism was associated with caste until I was in my forties; because my knowledge of how to be Indian is so tightly tied to my family, I do not have a broad range of caste practices for comparison. Essentially, on some level, for me, a blended heritage means that I do not know what aspects of my cultural makeup come from where, and I also often do not know what they mean.

Over the course of a lifetime, of course, we also all acquire culture—we move to new places, learn about them, are changed by them. I not only grew up a New England Unitarian, but I went to, and was changed by, a Quaker College outside of Philadelphia. That, and my deep affection for Philly—where I lived when I started these essays, are part of me. I lived for almost a decade in the American South, where I learned to love okra and converted to Judaism, both parts of my life (if one more important than the other) that have stayed with me. I am a knitter, a wannabe quilter, a dog person who lives with and loves a cat, a murderer of houseplants who has also managed to keep a fern alive for more than twenty-five years. I do not, in general, write about these pieces of my life here, in these essays—this is not, for instance, the story of my conversion to Judaism, or even about my life as (and scholarship about) a Jew of color or my love of Philly because it was such a good place (for me) to be a Jew of color, nor is it a book about how, though I am not a Quaker, a Quaker understanding of the world changed my approach to ethics. At times, however, those pieces of who I am peak through the stories that I am telling. Perhaps, someday, I will tell those stories, but for now, I mention them to give you context for the occasional mention.

The writing was slow, for any number of reasons, including the need to do the kind of writing for which I would (hopefully) receive tenure, but also because these essays have, at times, been painful to write. Indeed, there are topics that I have wanted to address and have put away for another time. Because I have written these essays over the years, in different political and personal moments, they also reflect different affective experiences of mixedness, of family, of home. I have chosen not to smooth out those differences in editing because, of course, they are all true. For instance, I have included both a nostalgic essay about where I am from, and an essay about the racism that I have experienced in various Connecticut suburbs. Both are true. And in the end, the nostalgia for home makes the racism painful in a particular and complicated way. I hope that, in having essays that express a range of experiences, I help to get at not only what it is to have mixed heritage, but also, in some small way, what it is to be human, to, as they say, contain multitudes.

One

WHERE ARE YOU
REALLY FROM? A TRIPTYCH

Where are you from?

W I am from a little tiny town, nestled up against a small city, both in the shadow of a ridge. In a lot of ways, my little town doesn't have much of an identity on its own, but in my little city, we make the best pizza in the world. My little city also has a stunningly high murder rate (the highest per capita in the country, I was told when I was growing up in the 1980s) and an Ivy League university, but as we dislike the murder rate and are, at best, ambivalent about the university, the pizza is really what we prefer to lead with. Even though I left home when I was eighteen, with such a deep desire to get out of Dodge that I did not even apply to our Ivy League university, and have never really even thought about going back to live there, my little city remains a center of my universe.

But where are you really *from?*

When I explain that, all right, I am not really from New Haven, I tell people that I am really from Woodbridge, a tiny town outside of New Haven, which had, in my childhood, about eight thousand people and still lacks a grocery store.

When I was growing up, you could not buy milk and eggs in Woodbridge between Thanksgiving and Easter, because the farm stands were closed. Now we have a year-round farm stand, but it is very toney—the kind of place where you can buy gourmet cheese and flatbread. You still have to go to New Haven, year-round, to buy toilet paper.

I always like people better when they accept my answer of where I am from, without asking a follow-up, because it means that they are engaging with me, as I experience myself, not as they want to experience me. (I once expressed a very snobby opinion about bagels while at a Rosh Hashanah dinner. The hostess, a lovely woman named Batya who had accepted me— the childhood friend of her second cousin's husband—at her table, asked where I was from. When I said New Haven, she nodded and said, "So, close enough to New York that you know a thing or two." I really liked her.)

When people accept my answer of where I am really from, I know that they are interested in knowing something about me rather than simply finding the answer that they are looking for. They are interested in the stories, landscape, and location that root me, even though it has been more than half my lifetime since I have routinely lived in the greater New Haven area.

When my friend Yoshimi came home with me, from grad school in Atlanta, to experience an American Thanksgiving, I took her on the nickel tour of New Haven. I think she wanted to go to the Beinecke to see a Guttenberg Bible. I, however, wanted to show her the New Haven that matters to me. We went by Claire's Corner Copia, the vegetarian restaurant where, in 1980, we would go for a treat if I was good during my mom's visits to the obstetrician and where, in junior high and high school, as a new vegetarian before it was easy or fashionable, I would do much of my hanging out. It is, as my friends in New

Haven would be happy to verify, one of my primary nostalgic meal sites, even now. We walked past Clark's, a family restaurant where, in 1982, my toddler sister drank ketchup straight from the bottle when the waitress took too long to get to us during a lunch rush. We went to the music school where, as a child, I wondered why people taking piano took lessons on the second floor while I had to carry my cello up to the third. We stopped in at Town Pizza (which serves Waterbury-style pizza, not New Haven–style pizza) to talk to Nick, the owner. When I was in junior high, I started having dinner at his counter once a week, in between my cello lesson and my chamber music trio. I would sit there and do my algebra homework, complaining that it was stupid, while he pointed out that he needed math every day to run his business. I sat at that counter every single week during the fall that I was applying to college. I left New Haven in 1996 and have lived in nine cities since then, and Nick always remembers where I am and what I am doing. He will probably buy this book, unless I give him a copy before he hears about it. Yoshimi wore out before I took her to other key sights—the store on Chapel where I got all my protest buttons and that my mother called a time warp, the burial excavation at the natural history museum that could give me nightmares up into my thirties, and the site of a favorite (and now absent) bookstore.

But what I remember most was Yoshimi's response to my whirlwind tour of my hometown. Yoshimi spent her childhood following her father's academic career. He was a grad student in Tokyo; a post-doc in Toronto; had, I think, at least one or two visiting positions before the family settled in the home where Yoshimi spent junior high and high school. She was amazed by the stories about me and my childhood that were woven into our tour of New Haven. She had thought she was going to see Yale, and yes, we went to visit the statue of Nathan Hale and the sculpture documenting the number of women at Yale through the ages (and a depressing sculpture it is, with its centuries of zeros), but her primary comment, as we drove back up the hill to my little village, outside of the city limits, was that she was amazed at how connected I was to this place, and how my memories layer on top of each other, from toddler me through adult me—now that she had seen me there, she said, she could not imagine that one could know me without knowing this place where I had been raised. And it struck her, she said, because she lacks that grounding in place. I left, and I am proud that I left and that I have seen more of the world, but New Haven and its suburbs remain very much where I am from.

When people do not accept my answer, it tends to be because of one of two desires on their part. One of which I am in sympathy with, but neither ever results in me giving the answer that they want, at least without some resentment.

South Asians ask me where I am from at as high a rate as white people, as it turns out—maybe higher. Not, I hasten to add, Asian Americans. We, that is, Americans who live outside the Black-white racial binary of the United States, know better than to ask people where they are from, at least without some sort of context for the question. South Asian immigrants, or visitors, however, ask all the time, I assume in some sort of search for connection. I have been asked where I am from by South Asian immigrants in places as disparate as on the A train from JFK to Brooklyn and in the Andover Theological Library of Harvard Divinity School, from (as those locations might imply) total strangers to new classmates.

It was my first week of Divinity School, and we were still in the phase where everyone was asking "where are you from?"

more or less all the time. I was finding the question fairly confusing. Many, if not most, people had relocated to Cambridge
to matriculate at the Div School, but I was twenty-four and had
moved to Cambridge two years before, when I had graduated
from college. But I was clearly a transient twenty-something. I
was not really from Cambridge. But I was also not really from
Swarthmore, Pennsylvania, where I had been to college, and I
was young enough to want to stake the claim of my adulthood
by not giving my parents' house as the answer to the question
where I was from. I had only barely been back for summers
since leaving for college. So, having lived in Cambridge for a
couple of years, I gamely said, "Right here."

"No, where are you really from?" asked my interlocutor, who
was, I knew, also a South Asian student, with an accent that
suggested immigrant.

"Oh," I said, "I was born about two hours from here."

"Oh," she asked, "but where are your parents from?"

And this is the point at which I get difficult. I have told you
where I am from and I know that random white people are not
asked where their family is from. So I answered, "My mother
is from Illinois."

And now she smelled blood. She honed in, "And your
father?"

This is the moment when I always want to say something
like, "Since he left us before I was born, why should I care?"
But I am loyal to my father, who did not leave before I was born
but, rather, took me trick-or-treating every year for the first
thirteen years of my life (and was devastated when, at thirteen,
I thought I was old enough to go with friends); supported my
mother in raising us on a steady diet of Pete Seeger and Su-
zuki music lessons; stole my "this is what a feminist looks like"
t-shirt from me, so that I would know that he was a feminist;

and did a remarkable job of adapting to the reality that his first-born, American daughter did not want to be a medical doctor but rather a doctor of philosophy. And so I allow her the information: he was born in Multan, but before Partition.

The phrase "before Partition" should have served as a warning to my interrogator, but instead, she said, "Your family is from Pakistan! So is mine!" And here, she actually gave voice to the point of her questions: "I knew we were the same!"

And here is the moment when I lost my cool. "If by just the same, you mean that your great-aunts and uncles literally hacked my people to bits with machetes and cost my family their land, their money, and their sanity, sure," I said. "We are the same. You could have let me be from New England, but if you are going to make me be South Asian, we are not the same. You are Pakistani, I am Indian, and your people are my enemy."

Not an attractive moment on my part. And not even true, in that I can only barely stand to interact with the uncles who were in the Indian army and believe that Muslims in general, and Pakistanis in particular, are the enemy. Precisely because they hold that view. But I also hate being boxed into an identity with which I do not want to lead, forced into connection that I do not feel, and to have all of that done as if it were not set in a number of complex geopolitical realities.

The search for connection, in other words, is tricky. I do not want to tell you that I am Indian in part because the culture that I bring to the table is rarely Indian. Or, at least, it is rarely Indian enough. All my life, I have associated my sense of not being Indian enough with my halfness, with the fact that 50 percent of my genes come from the British Isles, France, and Germany, and with the fact that my mother called many of the shots and created much of the cultural context of our home. My parents had a very traditional, very Indian division of labor—my father earned the bulk of the money, my mother ran the home and raised the children. And she raised us as cultural insiders to white, liberal, American Protestant culture. And so, I do not want to tell you that I am Indian and then, when you discover that I am, in the end, a Nutmegger, a New Englander to the core, have you tell me that I lack authenticity.

But here is the flip side of those questions—the side that is not about creating connection, however false. The "Where are you from" question in the hands of white people does an entirely different type of work.

When white people ask where I am from and press beyond my answer of "New England," it means they're saying, "You are not really from here." When you call them on this answer, they often explain that they are just curious and want to get to know you better. Because of the world in which I live, these white people are often well-meaning liberals, rather than people whose subtext is, ultimately, saying, "wherever you are from, it is not here and you should go home." I have worked in colleges, universities, and museums; worshipped in crunchy liberal Jewish and Unitarian communities; and almost always lived in hippie or hipster parts of town. I do everything I can to *not* encounter the people who would tell me that I need to "go back home."

Rather, the conversation goes something like this. I will be standing around, in some sort of cocktail-party or coffee-hour situation, chatting with people. I probably will not have asked them where they are from—maybe I know, or maybe I assume that we all live somewhere near the setting of this social engagement (a synagogue hall in Atlanta; a city library in Cambridge, Massachusetts; a hippie-dippie food co-op in Philadelphia).

As a result, I really do think that when white people ask me where I am "really" from, they are asking from a place of well-intentioned curiosity. They really do, somehow, feel that knowing my heritage will help them know me better, connect with me better. But what they are really doing, whether or not they realize it, is trying to control my story, how I tell it, and at what speed I tell it. And though they would be horrified to realize it, when they ask me where I am "really" from, but do not ask each other, they are also saying that, wherever I am from, the answer I have given, the answer of Woodbridge, of New Haven, of here (wherever that "here" might be), of the United States, is somehow implausible. I cannot be from the place where I was born, or the place where I pay rent or a mortgage, in the only country in which I have ever lived.

Khyati Joshi, an educator of educators at Fairleigh Dickinson University, calls this dynamic the "perpetual foreigner," and writes that the question "where are you really from" turns brown skin, the only "visible difference" between the questioner and the questioned, into "something that renders the latter less American." Since foreignness is stigmatized in American society, even the most well-intentioned set of questions, prompted by a genuine curiosity about the brown person's potentially fascinating background, creates a power imbalance that favors the white person in the exchange. It also, of course, presumes that the questioner has a right to determine someone else's narrative—that they have a right to personal details beyond those already shared.

This problem is such a common experience of life beyond the American Black-white binary (and something, I have been told, that sometimes happens to Black people as well) that you have almost certainly read other essays about the dilemma. There is even a hysterical (and at one time viral, at least among Asian

Americans) YouTube video of an Asian American woman getting asked where she is from by a random white guy while they are both out jogging. After a couple of comments about the weather, he asks her where she is from, since she speaks such perfect English. "San Diego," she responds. "We speak English there." He presses her on where she is really from—she was born in Orange County but eventually reveals that her great-grandmother was born in Seoul. Delighted to have what he wants, he responds with a greeting, perhaps in Korean, and some comments about kimchi and other foods, some of which are exactly as authentically Korean as chop suey is authentically Chinese.

The beauty of the comedy sketch is that the Asian American jogger responds as I imagine we all do in our imaginations. She asks where her blond interlocutor is from. When he tells her that he is "just American," she asks if he is Native American. When he finally responds that his grandparents are from England, she responds with a monologue that includes words like "blimey" and "top o' the morning to you," which is to say that she manages to mix ridiculous parodies of both England *and* Ireland, a country with whom England has, shall we say, a long and very complicated history. And she does it all in an accent worthy of Dick Van Dyke's Bert in the film version of *Mary Poppins*. And, even better, the sketch depicts the cluelessness of the white jogger. He thinks she is crazy and never does realize that she has just done to him what he had done to her.

The video is amazing. Because this is precisely what happens all the time. (And, no, I know that you love to eat naan, but I do not eat naan at home. First of all, Indian bread is a pain in the ass to make, much easier when you have servants [or a wife or a daughter-in-law, which, at least for my grandfather, was just another way of saying servants]. But more to the point, naan is usually not home bread. It requires a special oven. "We" eat chapatis at home.)

Of course, as my crack about naan suggests, the answer that people are looking for, when they ask me where I am really from, or where my family is from, is India. They want to know why I am brown, and the answer of India also confirms that I am wonderfully exotic. But as an answer itself, India is problematic at best as well.

First of all, I do not know India well. It was far removed from me, and from my own sense of self, a reality that my parents figured out when I was extremely small. My India was, until I was in my twenties, utterly imagined. Over the years, it has been imagined with ridiculous levels of inaccuracy. For instance, during my childhood, my mother did a lot of sewing, and we would occasionally go to Westport, Connecticut, where there was a particularly good fabric store. And when we went to this high-end fabric store, we would make something of an outing of it, stopping for lunch at Gold's Delicatessen. Gold's is, as I recently discovered on a nostalgia visit, an old-style, actually Kosher restaurant, a fleishig place with not a scrap of dairy in the building. It is so old school that each table has a cruet of schmaltz, rendered chicken fat, to schmear on toast, and when one sits down, the waiters bring you a bowl of kosher dills and half-sour pickles. During a visit when I was probably three or so, my toddler hand shot out toward the bowl. My mother realized that I thought that the pickle was a cucumber and warned me, "That cucumber is actually a pickle and it might be too, too sour."

I bit down and said, in a piercing little-kid voice, "Mommy! The pickle is not too, too sour!" And with that, I had charmed the waitstaff, grandfatherly men all, who started bringing me all sorts of treats. Pretzels and slices of sausage. I loved the deli. I even loved the chopped liver.

About two weeks later, my father and I were playing with the globe in the family room while my mother was cooking dinner. He must have decided to show me where he had grown up and where my grandfather lived because I excitedly clambered up the stairs. "Mommy, Mommy! Daddy, showed me on the globe, where Papaji lives!" And then my face went blank. I had forgotten the word. "What was the name of the place where the pickles were not too sour?"

And that was when my parents realized: I remembered the grandfatherly men at the deli, and when my father told me that my grandfather lived in Delhi, I knew just where he was. I just assumed that my Hindu, vegetarian grandfather worked in a *fleischadik* deli. It was, perhaps, the first hint that anyone got that I had almost no context for India.

Later, my parents watched the *Masterpiece Theatre* series *The Jewel in the Crown*, based on the books by Paul Scott, detailing the final years of the British Raj. Being, as it was, a BBC production, the primary point of view was British, so perhaps they did not offer the best insight into the India of my own family. We, after all, were the colonized, no matter how upper caste and middle class, not the colonizer. My primary memory of that series is a moment when the British mother, driven mad by her exile in India, with its foreignness and its climate, puts her baby in a circle of fire, with a scorpion. I believe, based on my hazy memories, that her goal is to kill the baby so as to save it from a life in India. The British version of the American "Mammy," the baby's ayah, her nanny, throws down her shawl to make a path through the flames, and rescues the child. My memories of these shows are hazy, but they were my earliest impressions of India and they mean that, to this day, I imagine

India lit with the lighting of a Merchant Ivory film, hazy and golden in its sense of heat. I do this despite the fact that, as an adult, I just chose to describe the ayah as akin to a Mammy figure—a sacrificial stereotype that has nothing to do with the experiences of the actual women raising their oppressors' children, and I wonder now, when it is too late to ask him, why my father wanted to watch this show that depicted India through British eyes.

I have been to India now, and I know that Delhi is not a Jewish deli, and I realize that there are many Indias other than the ones shaped by the combined forces of Merchant Ivory and the BBC, but it is still an imagined place for me. I am not from India.

But people do not want my story as I choose to tell it—they want the information that will satisfy either their quest for connection or their curiosity, and I know this, because I know their next question.

But where are your parents from?

Once again, the correct answer here, the one for which people are fishing, is, in the end, India. But this answer is not only problematic because I first went to India at twenty-four, for what has proved my only visit. It is also not that I have all the dislocation expressed by so many ABCDs (American Born Confused Desis). It is that India, is, at best, a crappy descriptor for my family's history. It erases my mother's heritage from my story, but it also collapses my father's family history into a sound bite that actually obscures much of how we, as a family, work.

First, to ask where my father was "really" from obscured important aspects of how he understood himself and the choices that he had made. My father was not an idiot. When people asked him where he was from, he knew what they were asking.

But he also felt very strongly that he had given up quite a bit in order to choose where it was that he wanted to live, and, at some point, that he had lived in Connecticut far longer than he had lived anywhere else in the world. And so, when he was asked where he was from, his answer depended on context. If we were in the state, but not in our actual town of Woodbridge, he would answer "Woodbridge." Anywhere else in country, he would answer "New Haven." In Canada, he would say "Connecticut." Of course, in India, no one ever asked him where he was from, but he enjoyed telling people that he was from outside of New York. And interestingly, the reason people in India did not ask him where he was from (or ask me either) was that they could tell. Our clothing, our body language, my tendency to mouth off and my father's tendency to let me, told everyone that we were from the United States.

When my father was dying, it became completely clear, though, that he was not simply claiming to be from Connecticut because he did not like answering questions about his immigration status. Hindu tradition says that one should put cremated remains in the Ganges river. When my uncle died, my aunt decided to keep his ashes in Massachusetts, putting some in the Charles River and burying the rest in Mount Auburn Cemetery, where my young cousins could visit their father. But while we therefore had family precedent for keeping ashes in the United States, my mother wanted my father to know that she would take his ashes back to India, if he wished her to do so. My father looked at her, with his big eyes, bleached blue with age and clouded with confusion, and said, "Why do you want to send me away from my home?" Connecticut, not India, had become home to my father. And so, if the question "Where are you from" is a question about where you root your life, where the center of your universe lies, then he was from our little brown house, in our little town, next to the little city where he assumed he would die in the same hospital in which his girls had been born.

My father rooted his life in our little brown house in Southern New England, but at least part of why he was open to a new home is that, before he rooted himself in Connecticut, he was a displaced person.

From late elementary school until he moved to Connecticut at thirty-one, my father lived in New Delhi, but that was not the country listed as his place of birth on his passport. My father was born in 1940, in the city of Multan, which is now in Pakistan. His family was Hindu. My grandfather worked for the British government. The British knew that Partition was coming, and so they transferred Hindu civil servants to what was going to be India, and Muslim civil servants to what was going to be Pakistan. By the time partition came, in 1947 when my dad was seven, my grandparents, my father, and his older brother had already relocated to Shimla, the summer capital of the British Raj, which is in India. And he would never see Multan again.

My father's immediate family were not in the parades of refugees that you see when you watch movies like *Gandhi*, but many of their relatives were. My grandfather had one sister. My grandmother had a sister and three or four brothers. When Partition happened, all of these siblings had spouses and children. They had scores of cousins. My grandparents had to find space for many of those people in their home in Shimla. My father told a story about the day that his mother took him to the train station to meet a train that had some of his uncles on it, coming from Multan. When they got to the station, a train from Pakistan was pulling in. The doors opened, and my father watched as blood poured out of the train. Muslims wielding machetes had massacred all the people on the train, all of whom were Hindus headed for the Indian side of the border. (Somewhere, on the Pakistani side of the border, I can only imagine that a different seven-year-old boy saw the same thing, when a train from India arrived filled with slaughtered Muslims, killed by Hindus with every bit as much horror.) My dad's uncles were not actually among the dead on that train—they arrived on the next train. Was this story true, or was it a childhood nightmare created by newsreels, overheard snippets of adult conversation, and violence in the streets? I do not know, but late in his life, when my father started to have dementia, I was at home in Connecticut, taking care of him while my mother was away and, unnerved by her absence, he worried that she was on a train and would be killed.

My grandfather was the only surviving son of a high-caste, land-owning family. All the land and the people who farmed that land were left behind when my father's family left for India. While my father's family was given new land on the Indian side of the border, essentially in trade for what they had given up, it was nowhere near as good—it did not have the same water, it was not as fertile. My father told stories of his farm, lost to us forever. In these stories, the land was beautiful and perfect. These family stories are, essentially, oral histories. And as someone who uses oral histories in my own research, I can tell you that they are often not accurate—if by accurate you mean strictly, factually correct. What that means is that when I tell you that I grew up hearing that the family land stretched from eight miles south of Kabul, in what is now Afghanistan, to Multan, which is in Pakistan, I have no idea if that is true, any more than I am certain that my father saw evidence of a train massacre. But here is the thing about that kind of family story. In some ways, it does not matter how much land there was, or whether my great-grandfather, who was the landowner, really sat on a dais to mediate disputes between the people who lived and worked on the land. (In other ways, it matters hugely—I do not want to ignore either the caste or class politics here, but I have to admit that I also do not fully understand them and cannot separate out what was true from what was family myth, made up by people with different politics than mine.)

What matters for this story is that for my dad and his older brother, that lost land took on immense meaning. An injustice had been done and nothing in their lives could ever replace what was gone. My father felt wronged. He longed for a farm, and he would forever mourn his family's. A part of him would always feel displaced. He wanted to see Multan and his farm one last time before he died. As Mira Kamdar writes in her memoir, *Motiba's Tattoos*, about a different moment of Indian exile, "To be an exile is to endure the unstoppable pain of separation from a land to which one is forbidden to return." My father applied for a visa multiple times, to the country listed as his birthplace on his passport, and was denied each and every time by the Pakistani government, presumably because, while his US passport said he had been born in Pakistan, he had once held Indian citizenship. The older he became, the more painful these denials were to him.

When people ask where I am "really from," they are fishing for an answer to explain why I look different—where "different" simply means brown and therefore not American—and the answer of India is deeply satisfying to them, but, in reality, though my father spent much of his childhood and young adulthood in New Delhi, and while it was the scene of many important memories and crazy college stories, it was neither where he was born nor a place that he had chosen. It was home, but it was not really home. It was always a place of exile, while the mythic farm, far north in the Panjab, on the Pakistani side of the border, was home.

You would think, then, that one way to address the question of "where are you really from" would be to say that my family is really from Pakistan. But, as anyone who knows people who were displaced by Partition could probably tell you, that would not be an acceptable answer. My father's US Passport listed his place of birth as Multan, Pakistan, even though when he was born, the nation state of Pakistan did not exist. And my father has never set foot in the nation-state of Pakistan, which has been, for every single moment that the two countries have existed, India's enemy. For all my father often liked, and wanted to hang out with, Pakistani Muslims in the US, sharing, as they did, a language, a love of Urdu poetry and communal poetry readings, and a culinary tradition, I think it would be fair to say that he actively and actually hated the country of Pakistan, its government, and the idea that its creation had cost him his home. Pakistan is most definitely not where my father was from.

But my mother is from somewhere too.

The other problem, of course, if you are me and you are mixed, is that, if my ancestry is where I am "really" from, to ask about my father's heritage, the heritage written on my skin, denies a full half of my ancestry and a very real aspect of my experience. You see, it is not that I am self-hating as an Indian American or as a person of color. It is just that I am my mother's daughter. I am my mother's daughter for many reasons. Some of them are about the internal dynamics of my family. My mother, and not my father, controlled our world and its culture, and so I was raised primarily on Laura Ingalls Wilder and *Anne of Green Gables*, Madeleine L'Engle and Louisa May Alcott. We went to my mother's church and learned more of her family recipes. And also, while I loved my father madly, he was certainly the more unpredictable parent, alternately a delightful playmate and a source of real fear. My mother was my source of comfort—the person I identified with, defining myself in relationship to her.

My mother is from Rockford, Illinois, which is known for manufacturing hammers. She went to Oberlin College. For most of my childhood, she strongly identified with the Midwest, though she has lived in our house in Woodbridge longer than she lived in the Midwest, and has lived in Connecticut for twenty years longer than she has lived in our house. She only came to Connecticut because, at twenty years old, she met a guy at a wedding. He was interesting, he was older, he was Indian, and when she graduated from college, she followed him to where he lived, to Connecticut, and, ironically, to the seat of her family's history.

My mother told me more of the stories of who we were— she was even the keeper of my father's family stories. I was raised on my Great-Great-Aunt Clara's baking powder biscuits and my Great-Grandma Turcott's pumpkin pie. Every year, I avoided the fruitcake, made with fruit from my Grandpa Hotchkiss's company, Edenfruit, in Poplar Grove, Illinois. I have two middle names, the first of which is my mother's middle name and her mother's first name. My mother raised me on Unitarian hymns and taught me to light a menorah, saying the blessings with an Ashkenazi accent. I knew that, when my mom was growing up, her Jewish grandfather would let her have four little cups of sweet wine at the Passover seder, which horrified her mother, who had been raised in a culture shaped by the Women's Christian Temperance Union. I grew up with stories of women almost dying in childbirth on the family farms in upstate New York, where soldiers buried treasure before leaving for the Civil War. And so, when I think of my ancestors, I am more likely to think of my mother's family than my father's. In some ways, my mother's ancestors' may seem more real to me than they do to her, because while she grew up in the Midwest, I am from New England. I was born only a couple of miles from my maternal ancestor's family's point of entry into what would become the United States.

My mother's maiden name first appears in the records of the New Haven Colony in 1641, when my first ancestors in the American colonies appeared in court. Samuel Hotchkiss and Elizabeth Cleaverly were both underage and lacked proof of their parents' consent for their marriage, but according to the court records, as they had "entred into contract, sinfully and wickedly defiled each other with filthy dalliance and uncleane passages, by which they have both made themselves unfitt for any other and for which they have both received publique correction, upon these considerations, granted them liberty to marry." As their son John was baptized in 1643, and as New England Puritans were generally speaking more concerned with bastardy than with premarital sex, it is likely that the couple married because Elizabeth was pregnant. (Baptism, for those early New Englanders, could occur right after birth but did not necessarily do so. And, of course, John could have followed an earlier baby who died, unrecorded.)

Our family history is intimately tied up with New Haven, where I grew up—Westville, the New Haven neighborhood that borders my hometown of Woodbridge, used to be called Hotchkissville—or at least so one uncle claimed, not randomly, but after my ancestors. (I am not sure about this—contemporary maps place Hotchkissville a short distance away, in Woodbury.) While we are from a different branch of the family than the one that endowed the Hotchkiss School, one of Connecticut's prep schools, we are close enough kin to end up at Hotchkiss Family Association gatherings with them, in the town of Prospect, Connecticut, also a scant twenty minutes from where I grew up.

When my friend Ben stayed with me at my parents' house, as we road-tripped from Boston to Atlanta, he told me that, since it was snowing, he wanted to see a postcard New England church. I showed him the church in the center of my hometown, and while it is lovely, with white clapboard and a steeple, it lacks a graveyard. So we drove ten minutes up the road to the next town. We stopped at my junior high school on our way, since we were taking a tour of my childhood, and then drove up to the First Congregational Church of Bethany, Connecticut. I stayed in the car, muttering about tourists and Texans, while Ben walked through the falling snow to the churchyard. At which point he decided I was punking him. He wiped off the first stone that he came to and my mother's maiden name (which he knew, as it is the second of my middle names) was carved on the stone. But he was also, I think, sort of amazed by my little towns and by the fact that our lives were intertwined with those of our ancestors. My mother has not decided what to do with my father's ashes, but one of her favorite possibilities is another graveyard, this one in our town, where more Hotchkisses are buried, and where a family of wild turkeys makes their home.

That is how I tell the story, in my head, of my home and my connection to New Haven—and the story of my mom, moving back to her ancestor's original New England home because she met a guy from India at a wedding in Pittsburgh. I like the arbitrariness. My father ended up in Connecticut for no real reason—he followed a job. But he could have gone to Pittsburgh from anywhere in the US, and my mom would have followed him there. But instead, somehow, randomly, though it feels fated, I was raised in a place steeped in my family history.

But, of course, we do not really know where Samuel and Elizabeth came from—Essex is what the ship's manifest lists, at least for Sam, but lots of ships left from Essex, and there is no guarantee that is where he was really from. And as I sat in a Philadelphia restaurant with a fellow half-Asian New Havenite, entrusted to read early drafts of these essays, he commented on the ways in which colonialism has shaped both sides of my family story—that mine is a family story structured, on both sides, by different kinds of British colonialism. And of course, my friend was right, and he was generous in pointing out that there are reasons why I do not tell my story this way—it is not, he said, like I grew up in Colorado, New Mexico, or South Dakota, where there are reservations and Indigenous communities that are clearly marked. Rather, Connecticut is what settler colonialism looks like at its most "successful." While there are most certainly Indigenous communities in Connecticut, they are not part of our consciousness, other than in a few place names, here and there, and the Foxwoods Casino with its attendant museum. We do not have to think about how we came to have this land, and so we do not. To be Indian, from India, is to never be able to forget the English. To be descended from the English, in New England, is to be able to forget. The contrast is striking.

Neither my mother, nor her parents, grew up in Connecticut, but I did, surrounded by my family's history, with a sense that I belonged to this land where my ancestors were buried. And so, when people ask where I am really from, it gets to me, to know that they want the history of my Indian ancestors, who lived lives that I can barely imagine, and somehow discount the ancestors whose histories were intertwined with my childhood.

This family history ties me to place, but so does the deep familiarity of home. I have now been to India and, while it is fascinating, to me it is foreign. When I think of foreign, I think of fruit. When I was a little kid, whenever my Indian uncles came to visit from Boston, they and my dad would take the train into New York City to go to Chinatown and buy a crate of mangos. They would bring them home, take the washtub that my mom bought for apple-bobbing, fill it with ice, and chill down the mangos. All afternoon, we would sit on the patio, eating mangos, and they would tell my sister and me about how these mangos were nothing, compared to the mangos at home. There were so many kinds of mangos at home. But we only ever had one or two kinds, and to me they were a treat, and an effort and an event. Meanwhile, for the forty years that my father spent in New England, the fall apples were a miracle—an exotic fruit, literally falling off the tree in our backyard, available from orchards all over the place. Growing up in India, apples had been a rare treat for him. For me, however, apples are both infinite in their variety and completely standard. I am writing this in January. It is not apple season, but my local grocery store still has eight kinds of (mostly) local apples in stock. I know the varieties with the same exactness that my father knew mangos, and I love them all, and yet they are not special. They are to be eaten with peanut butter when I am too tired to cook. To be Indian is to know mangos in all the varieties that I cannot name; to be a New Englander is to know Winesap or Brayburn or Pink Ladies. And I am a New Englander.

And that sense of history and place, my own, but also my family's, makes me always want to answer the question of "where are you from" by saying, quite simply, that I am from New Haven, this place that has so deeply shaped me. If they wanted to really know who I am, they would let me answer, "I am from a little tiny town, nestled up against a small city, both in the shadow of a ridge. In a lot of ways, my little town doesn't have much of an identity on its own, but in my little city, we make the best pizza in the world."

Two

MEAT IS MURDER

I have never worn a "Meat Is Murder" t-shirt to Thanksgiving dinner. Clearly, I have thought about doing it, and while I would like to be able to claim that I have not done so because it would be rude or because I have deep-seated reservations about Morrissey, really, I have not done so because I have never been quite enough of a Smiths' fan to have ever made the jump from buying CDs to buying t-shirts.

Thanksgiving, however, has always been a challenge for me. And it is possible that I wish, on some level, that I had the t-shirt and the ability to be that rude.

I know vegetarians and vegans who have different attitudes toward being the culinary outsiders. Some really do not seem to mind it. I have a friend who has made it through many years in Rome as a lactose intolerant vegetarian who does not drink, and he has yet to complain about anything culinary except for the crappy quality of Italian tea. To be honest, even though I am something of a foodie, I am happy to work around meat in any number of ways. I travel with peanut butter, so that I can navigate communal meals and entire countries that include meat-heavy cuisines. But particularly at Thanksgiving, there is something about the communal meal that feels communion-like. And I mind being excluded. I mind the sense that my extended family is more careful and respectful of people who are gluten-free than they are of my vegetarianism, and that sometimes the gluten-free people are the least respectful of my vegetarianism.* I really mind the amount of work that I end up doing to create a meal that I won't fully be a part of, and I mind that it goes on for days, as all ten or more of us eat leftovers and people talk about how there is no need to actually cook new food.

One year, I decided that rather than being crabby, I would be proactive. In my family, the meat-based traditions continue on to the day after Thanksgiving, when, for more than a decade, my uncle made a turkey gumbo for the entire family. The gumbo was not as much of a production as the actual Thanksgiving dinner, but it was close. We made homemade stock from the turkey carcass, picking off as much of the meat as possible, to add to the soup later. The stock simmered all night, it had to be strained, and then we made the gumbo. Inevitably, making the roux filled the house with smoke. We had to open doors, letting in the cold, raw November air. It was a production—a big family social event, one that neither I nor the aunt with celiac disease could enjoy. (This aunt is, however, a more laidback person than I am. If she minded, she never let on.) And so I decided to make an entire stock pot of red lentil soup, enough for anyone who wanted some, almost in hopes that my big pot

---

*Two points: First, I am not sure that the gluten-free people feel like they are more accommodated than I am, but they certainly feel more free to ban bread from the meal for everyone than I feel to ban the Thanksgiving turkey. And second, ironically, the aunt who actually has celiac disease is both the most accommodating of me and the least likely to force us all into her ways of eating, even though she is the one with the most dire need to do so.

of soup would create a way for me (and my gluten-free aunt) to participate, if not in the communal dish, in the meal, rather than simply microwaving the next round of leftovers.

I made the soup ahead of time and pulled it out once the gumbo was made (and the turkey grease that films the kitchen by the end of the process was scrubbed away). And come time to serve, the two soups sat, side by side, bubbling away on a nice clean stove next to a pot of rice. Each with its own ladle.

One of my non-celiac aunts and I were next to each other, by the stove. She was helping herself to soup and I was getting out spoons, when I watched her take the ladle from the gumbo and pour a serving of gumbo onto the rice in her bowl. I then watched, and somehow did not manage to stop her, as she took the gumbo ladle, dipped it into the lentil soup, and made a parallel stripe of lentil soup alongside.

And all of a sudden, I could no longer eat the soup. It was as unacceptable, as treyf, to me as it would have been if made with a ham bone.

I had an intense (and entirely internal) emotional reaction: I was frustrated. I had planned ahead. I had solved a problem. And I watched my solution evaporate through someone else's thoughtlessness. I was also furious. I almost cried, I felt so fundamentally disrespected.

My aunt, who had no idea that anything was wrong, turned to me, still holding the meat ladle, and asked if I wanted rice for my lentil soup. I explained that I thought I would have a peanut butter sandwich instead. She was understandably confused—why had I made this big pot of soup? I had to explain that, when she put the ladle into the lentil soup, it had stopped being vegetarian, and so I was no longer comfortable eating it.

"What are you now?" she asked. "Some kind of religious fanatic?"

I stared at her in horror. She had ruined my meal without a thought. And yet somehow I was the difficult one? But it is also interesting that she identified my vegetarianism as being fundamentally religious. That is not how I would have framed what I was doing, but the more I have thought about her response, and my own experience of meat—as food, as raw material, as dead animal—the more I realize that she was seeing something about me that frustrated and baffled her, something that separates me from the relatives (including the vegetarians) on the American side of my family, and something that deeply informs the hows, if not precisely the whys, of my vegetarianism.

I first became a vegetarian when I was four, when I made the connection between lamb on the plate and the lambs that had just been born at our local farm museum. Previously, I had not known of animal words that matched food words. I knew the words "hen" and "rooster," but had somehow missed that together, they were chicken, just like the food on my plate. But as soon as I realized that lamb-the-food was also lamb-the-animal, I connected all the dots and stopped eating meat at all. I do not remember any of this. But according to my mother, I lasted about six months, which, one must admit, shows real determination for a four-year-old. The primary problem was that I was four—I did not eat enough other foods besides meat. I was willing to eat toddler white foods: bread and pasta. My mother gamely baked all sorts of milk and eggs and vegetables into bread. But she was also very relieved when I came to the conclusion that, as the Thanksgiving turkey was very big, perhaps it had died of old age. "Perhaps it did," she reports that she told me. And I ate meat for another seven years, though there was another sticky moment when I read *Charlotte's Web*.

My brief stint as an omnivore ended for good when I was twelve and I went to visit one of my mother's sisters, an aunt who lives too far away to come to family Thanksgiving dinners and was, at the time, vegetarian. She and her boyfriend were both twenty-four, an age more interested in accuracy and ideology than in getting nutrients into picky children, and when my aunt found out my meat-dies-of-old-age theory, she set me straight. And I have not eaten a land animal since. (I flirt, periodically and uncomfortably, with pescatarianism—mostly when I lived in Atlanta and found life so much easier if I was willing to eat fish, but I have almost never cooked it in my own home.)

If you were to talk to me about what informs my dietary choices, I would sound like any other liberal American vegetarian. I would talk about the inhumane treatment of animals, and about the environmental impact of eating meat. If you countered these arguments with comments about how eating much less, much more ethically raised meat solves these problems, I would point out that, no matter how happily the Thanksgiving turkey was raised, it still ends up dead on the plate, so at the very best, free-range, "happy" meat ameliorates the problems but does not fully solve them. But if I was feeling particularly obstreperous and the date was close to Thanksgiving, I might also explain that, at least in the case of turkeys, ethical is not really one of the options on the table. Very few turkeys are raised on pastureland, and all domesticated turkeys are artificially inseminated at the time that will allow them to be at full weight for Thanksgiving. Turkeys, I would note, do not like to be artificially inseminated.

But even if I was not feeling argumentative, I might start talking about how much I love my dogs and cat, and how I assume that, if I knew cows as intimately as I know my animals, I would have similarly intimate relationships with them. In the end, all my reasons for being vegetarian are rooted in the intellectual framework of animal rights and environmentalism, along with a conviction that, however much of a soul humans have, animals have every bit as much of one. Not eating meat comes from the same set of impulses as watching whether my clothing comes from sweatshops, buying fewer things made more ethically, or the myriad ways in which I try to live such that I harm other people as little as possible. Just as I fail there, for any number of reasons, I fail here—my logic should lead me to be vegan, but I am both kind of lazy and exceedingly fond of cheese.

In my extended family, however, my sensibilities about contamination also cast me, in some subtle way, as the family problem, a killjoy who would not participate in the family fun.

The idea of the killjoy comes from the writing of Sara Ahmed, who wrote both "A Killjoy Manifesto" and "A Killjoy Survival Kit," both of which appear in her book *Living a Feminist Life*. Though I have never met her, I feel particular kinship with Ahmed because, like me, she grew up with a South Asian father and a white mother, in her case, in Australia. In *Living a Feminist Life*, she writes compellingly about the realities of being brown in a white, settler colonial state, while also not being part of the Pakistani immigrant communities. While she does not directly connect the concept of the feminist killjoy to being the mixed child of a Pakistani father and a white mother, when she writes of her childhood status as a feminist killjoy, she sets the term in that context before going on to write: "When you name something as sexist or racist you are making that thing more tangible so that it can be more easily communicated to others. But for those who do not have a sense of the racism or sexism you are talking about, to bring them up is to bring them into existence." This is particularly important because, as she puts it, "when you expose a problem, you pose a problem."

While the idea killjoy is not explicitly linked to being mixed, I wonder if it resonates for me in part because she frames it in a family similar to mine. For Ahmed, like for me, her identity as a killjoy began at the dinner table. She talks about sitting at her family dinner table, with her parents and her two sisters, and pointing out the sexism that she heard at the table, and the emotion and distress that she felt at that sexism. The feminist killjoy, then, is not a problem simply because she points out sexism, but because she is upset by it. She takes a perfectly normal family discussion, about the prom, about fashion, about a friend's new boyfriend, and in exposing both the sexism in the conversation and her own distress at it, she makes the situation tense. She is a killjoy because the lovely family dinner, a space and occasion of joy, is now a sight of tension, of unpleasantness. And for everyone else sitting at the table, the unpleasantness is not because they had accepted and repeated sexist assumptions, but because she had pointed them out and been overwrought when she did so.

I grew up in a family in which feminism was taken for granted, even if, like all lived ideologies, that feminism was complicated. I was, instead, a vegetarian killjoy. Many people, many foodies, see vegetarians as killjoys because we prioritize something over the pure enjoyment of food. Perhaps that something is health, perhaps animal rights, perhaps environmentalism. But the fact that something is being held up over and against the pleasures of food, the sensory joys of a good meal, but also the communal nature of the meal and the open and uncritical acceptance of hospitality, makes us killjoys. Anthony Bourdain famously wrote, in the *New Yorker* essay that launched his career, "Vegetarians, and their Hezbollah-like splinter-faction, the vegans, are a persistent irritant to any chef worth a damn. To me, life without veal stock, pork fat, sausage, organ meat, demi-glace, or even stinky cheese is a life not worth living. Vegetarians are the enemy of everything good and decent in the human spirit, an affront to all I stand for, the pure enjoyment of food." For Bourdain, the killjoy was something worse than a downer. It was opposed to simple human decency.

Sometimes my killjoy status was really primarily logistical. On my mother's side of the family, the white side, my vegetarianism was always treated as reasonable, but those logistics still made me a killjoy. I was the person who needed a separate entrée at holiday dinners, and there was always tension. If they made only enough for me, some sort of special treat, I was rude if I did not share or if I objected as my meal was passed around the table—watching as the possibility of seconds evaporated. If they made enough for everyone, it added expense and work to the meal for the hosts, who might have also roasted a turkey. Other times, particularly when I was younger and more the kind of person who might have shown up in a "meat is murder" t-shirt, my killjoy qualities were more likely to come out in comments about animal suffering or environmentalism. But even if I am simply asking that people respect my boundaries and keep their meat spoons out of my vegetarian dishes, as far as my family is concerned, I am something of a problem.

As my family members on the Indian side have become enthusiastic meat eaters with their move to the United States, I have become a killjoy to them as well. Perhaps even more of a killjoy, as my vegetarian presence may serve as a reminder that they are transgressing. An uncle once explained that it is impossible to be vegetarian in the United States, and therefore silly to try (and rude to make them accommodate me). "Even those pastries you are eating," he commented, "were probably made with lard. There is no way to know!" And honestly, they might well have been, I suppose. As a high school student, I was not yet the kind of vegetarian who would have known or thought to ask, though of course one always can ask. I have always found it weird that my Indian aunts and uncles, several of whom like to harp on all the ways that I am not Indian enough also criticize my vegetarianism, although it is the most Indian thing about me, and this is part of why I understand my vegetarianism as a killjoy problem, in Ahmed's sense. It reminds everyone that they are doing wrong. It reminded the liberal Unitarians of their ethical failures around animal cruelty and environmentalism. It reminded the Indian relatives that they were being bad Hindus and therefore bad Indians, not so much because they believed strongly in the purity restrictions that govern our caste, but because their choices around assimilation sit uncomfortably with them and because, were she alive, their mother (who likely did believe in purity restrictions and caste) would be disappointed in them.

While I can point to any number of rational reasons for my vegetarianism, and while I am fully aware that the logical extension of these rational reasons is veganism, there is a deeply emotional and instinctive reaction fueling my vegetarianism. I do not want to eat anything that has touched meat. Or really, anything that has been touched by something that has touched meat. When I was in junior high school, my parents realized that we would need a separate grill for my vegetables and veggie burgers. And they got one, building two fires, every time we grilled out, keeping separate tongs and serving plates. And there are two things that are significant about my profound disgust—this sense of meat as contaminating, both of me and of anything that it has touched. First, I never thought about how accommodating my parents were of my insistence on strict separation, and perhaps therefore, I never thought about the fact that not everyone does vegetarianism the way that I do.

Second, I never thought about the fact that vegetarianism has not struck me as a sacrifice—in many ways, the revulsion came first, and the justification and reasons came later. Because I do not feel that revulsion towards many dairy products, I continue to eat them, an impulse that is supported by the little I know of Hinduism, in which milk is used to purify. And while that sensibility does not justify my not being a vegan, it goes a certain part of the way toward explaining it.

My aunt identified my rejection of meat and my sense that she had made my soup impure as "religious fanaticism." While I reject the idea that I am a fanatic, fundamentally, my revulsion at meat has religious qualities to it. My horror at meat, at things that have touched meat, or at the idea of consuming something derived from meat (gelatin, for instance) is, one could argue, religious.

And here is where my attitudes towards meat become interesting. For me, meat is utterly taboo, not only because its modes of modern production are an animal rights, labor rights, and environmental disaster, not even because it is dead, but because it horrifies me. Sometimes, even fake meat horrifies me.

When busy, I tend to be almost completely willing to live off soy-based chicken nuggets (and tater tots, but I'd rather not actually admit to that in public). I am fairly fond of fake breakfast sausage, and recently discovered a really good line of vegan sausages for other times of day. But for me, that is where the fake meat usually begins and ends. The Impossible Burger, and others of its ilk, are currently all the rage among many of my vegetarian friends, and I want to be excited about them. But though there are kinds of fake meat that I like, mostly fake sausage, the more perfectly fake meat approximates actual meat, the more difficult it is for me to eat it. I discovered this when I was out to dinner with a chemist friend of mine. We were in the little city where we were teaching and, surprisingly, a new local restaurant was serving the Impossible Burger. Ian wanted to try the restaurant and I wanted to try this hot new trend in vegetarian food. And when the burger showed up, it had flavors that I had not encountered in thirty years. Even though I basically do not remember what meat tastes like, something about this was familiar. And it was horrifying to me. I made Ian taste it, ostensibly because I can't remember what meat tastes like and I wanted to know if the burger really was an accurate facsimile, but really because I was afraid that I could remember what meat tasted like, that the kitchen had made a mistake, and that this burger really was meat.

Chemist that Ian is, and a person who teaches a course on the chemistry of cooking at that, he figured out that I was likely reacting to the iron. The Impossible Burger contains a large amount of iron, which is part of what makes it so very meat-like. The company is also, apparently, very careful with the fat content—it is that extra fat, combined with beet dye, that make the Impossible Burger, famously, "bleed." But whatever it was, that hamburger lit up the circuits in my brain that said meat—what I think of as the Mary Douglas circuits.

Early on in graduate school, I, like everyone else in my field, read the works of Mary Douglas, specifically a book called *Purity and Danger*, a text that is central for explaining how it is that people experience certain, arguably irrational, revulsions. Douglas was a cultural theorist and anthropologist who published *Purity and Danger* in 1966, and though over the course of her career she would adjust some of the specific examples in her book, deciding, for instance, that she had misunderstood the book of Leviticus, her broader arguments about how the concepts of purity, sacrality, impurity, and pollution operate across cultures has proved so influential that, in 1991, the *Times*

Literary Supplement included it in their one hundred most influential nonfiction books since 1945, alongside books such as Michel Foucault's *Madness and Civilization*, Carl Jung's *Memories, Dreams, Reflections*, E. P. Thompson's *The Making of the English Working Class*, and Clifford Geertz's *Interpretation of Cultures*. The feat is even more impressive when one realizes that Mary Douglas was one of only four women on this list. (The other three were Hannah Arendt, Jane Jacobs, and Simone de Beauvoir. If I were Betty Friedan, Rachel Carson, or Susan Sontag, I would be miffed to say the least.)

Basically, Douglas argues that what makes something pure or impure is essentially about boundary policing. The impure is something that is out of place—she uses the rules that determine what is kosher and what is not to make her argument (and as one of my graduate school professors said, one of the most impressive things about the argument is that she actually got the logic of kosher rules wrong but still created a theory that is completely and totally useful in thinking about purity and impurity).* Douglas argues that our ideas of what is dirty or defiling are symbolic, rather than strictly based in hygiene or logic. She points out that we, in the United States, do not think of shoes as dirty, but it is dirty to put them on a dining room table (and it is weird and unsettling to do so, even if they are never worn shoes straight out of the box). Food, likewise, is not dirty, but dirty dishes are a sign of filth when left in the bedroom in a way that they are not when left (for a reasonable amount of time) in the kitchen sink. Uncleanness, she argues, is "matter out of place," and to understand this is the "first step towards

---

*Note that she fixes some of her takes on kashrut in the introduction to her 2002 edition of the book, though that rendering is still sort of a strange take on kashrut.

insight into pollution." In Hinduism or Islam, you might not wear shoes into a temple or mosque because you should not defile sacred space, but (barring specific ceremonies like the foot washing of Maundy Thursday), Western Christians are similarly reluctant to be barefoot in church, because the feet themselves are unclean. Most importantly, there is not really a clear-cut distinction here between religious and secular. It might be a religious sense of impurity that drives one to bare or cover feet in a sacred space, but my Impossible Burger is also matter out of place. It is fake meat that is simply too convincing, too filled with flavors that no longer belong in my food—which is, of course, exactly the point of the Impossible Burger and the Beyond Burger—to let you eat meat without actually eating meat. I just don't want to.

The fact that the revulsion extends, for me, far beyond the intellectual politics of my food is, perhaps, best illustrated by my reaction to hunting. I grew up in the northeastern United States, a place that is more or less overrun by deer. In the spring, summer, and fall, deer corpses litter the sides of the highway. Herds of deer live in the woods in my parents' suburban neighborhood (though to be fair, it is a suburb of the wooded, two-acre-zoning variety). The deer are a problem for humans, in that they bring Lyme-carrying ticks and eat gardens, both vegetable and ornamental. Deer also, when hungry in the winter, strip the bark from trees, killing them. And the overpopulation of deer creates problems for the deer as well, largely when there is not enough food to go around in the winter. Barring a spay-and-release program, or the active reintroduction of nonhuman predators such as wolves into the suburbs, hunting really is a reasonable approach to the overpopulation of deer.

There are approaches to hunting that address most of my animal rights concerns as well, at least everything except the part whereby the animal is dead on a plate. One summer, I worked closely with a summer research student. She watched me as I built a syllabus on religion and food, with food justice as a major theme, and also as I navigated our deeply non-vegetarian-friendly summer dining options on campus. She read the food justice work on her breaks, and one day asked me what I thought, as a vegetarian, about hunting. My student, as it turns out, is a hunter. She learned from her father, who had taught all three of his daughters to hunt, and to do so without "spinning" the animal. Spinning, as she explained to me, means "shooting an animal incorrectly and traumatizing it to the point where it is in a state of suffering." When I asked about her thoughts on hunting, for this essay, she wrote, "The 'shot' part of hunting, at least in my Dad's eyes, was of the utmost importance to ensure you didn't put [the animal] through more pain than necessary," though she also realized that to me it might sound "a little weird, as you are intending to 'kill the animal without hurting it.'" She also wrote that she was raised to believe that you should use every single part of the animal possible. Ideally, she explained, that would mean absolutely everything, but "many hunters don't use all parts (this is partially an economic issue because unless you're professionally skilled in leather work it can cost thousands of dollars to have someone make those parts of the animal into something of use)." Most hunters, she wrote, do use everything that they can use for food. She told me that her family did not buy meat at the grocery store, as a single deer, along with some wild turkey, can feed her family of five for the entire winter, and that game can be substituted into most recipes. She closed her letter by noting that, "I feel better about not supporting the mass factory farming system where the process is inhumane and gives no consideration to the animal as a being."

So, if hunters are so closely aligned with my values, and my student's note indicates at least some of them are, why wouldn't I eat game? The answer, as it turns out, lies with my revulsion toward meat. In fact, the very last piece of mammal that I ever ate was deer. When I was in college, I belonged to a social group that was deeply dedicated to what I am fairly comfortably describing as gustatory hedonism. I was, I believe, the only vegetarian in the crowd, and while the other members of the group were nice enough about it, being Swarthmore students, they also definitely privileged taste over ethics. If we could have afforded foie gras, they would have had it on the table. Still, there were always vegetarian options for me, and I was rarely asked to foot the bill for the meat. One of the guys in the group was from rural New Jersey and had grown up in the woods. A neighbor hunted deer on his family land and provided his family with some of the meat. For him, venison, particularly a stew that his family made, was heritage food. So here we were, in this social group that was so defined by food, and at one point, he brought back the venison stew to have a dinner with the group. I arrived a day too late to go to the dinner, but when I got back to campus, I found out that he had saved a serving for me. He knew that I was a vegetarian, but also realized that most of my concerns did not apply to venison. And it really, really mattered to him that I try his stew. So I did. I had a bite. I do not remember what it tasted like, but I remember his smile and remember thinking that I was doing this because sharing food is communion. He was so happy, and then he flitted away, and as soon as I thought about what I had done, I vomited, and continued to do so sporadically all evening. This was not biology. While vegetarians sometimes find meat overly rich, it takes decades of vegetarianism to starve off the gut flora that help you digest meat, and since I was (and am) vegetarian and not vegan, I do eat other kinds of animal protein. I was not vomiting because my body could not handle it, but because I kept thinking about how gentle the eyes of a fawn are, and how lovely deer are leaping through the woods.

Of course, though, these things are both deeply cultural and also subjective. In a lunchtime conversation, over a shared vegetarian pizza, my friend Katie tells me that she serves her family Beyond Burgers (the primary competitor of the Impossible Burger) for dinner at least once a week. Katie is a pescatarian, and from a logical standpoint, her reasons for being one are very much like mine. She writes that she has always come from what she refers to as a "Peter Singer type reasoning," by which she means that, like the Princeton professor and moral philosopher, she is concerned that the modern, Western system of meat production manages to be cruel to animals, devastating to the environment, and unhealthy for the people eating meat, and also, perhaps, that she sees the lines between humans and animals as somewhat arbitrarily drawn. All of Katie's logical reasons for avoiding meat match mine.

From an affective standpoint, however, her response to meat is very different from mine. She loves the taste of beef, and correspondingly, of the Beyond Burger. If Katie loves meat, it horrifies me. It is impure, as I said, and that revulsion is much of what fuels my own avoidance of meat.

In many ways, as someone steeped in Calvinist cultures of discipline, I have more respect for her vegetarianism than for mine, because of the sacrifice involved—she is not repulsed by meat, she is morally concerned by it and therefore abstains. I am morally concerned by it, but apparently, my repulsion extends beyond meat to things that are "meat-like," that remind me, in some sensory way, of meat. The same miracles of technology that make these substitutes thrilling for people who abstain for purely moral reasons repulse me, making me not quite their demographic.

Shortly after the Thanksgiving when my aunt contaminated my vegetarian soup, my mother and I were talking about what had happened—my aunt, I think, had complained to my mother about how rude I had been as they planned for Christmas. My aunt felt that I should have eaten the soup anyway, been more concerned with being a host—with breaking bread together—than with my own horror. My mother, a Unitarian in the rational humanism school of that tradition, reflected that my attitude toward vegetarianism might come from my early training in Hinduism.

According to my mother, one of the earliest lessons she taught me, as part of living in Indian communities, was to never, ever move a spoon from one dish to another, ever. While she did not, as far as I know, explain why you do not move a spoon from one dish to another, it was an essential skill for functions. In this case, functions are the parties described in Jhumpa Lahiri's *The Namesake*, crowded parties, in suburban homes or, sometimes in rented rec centers. These parties usually featured big aluminum foil trays of food, either made ahead by the hostess or catered in. You would move down the buffet table, with potentially a tray or two of chicken mughlai, a couple of choices of dal, and a couple of sabji, or vegetable. For many Hindu vegetarians, if you were to move the serving spoon from the chicken into the dal or the vegetables, they would then be rendered "non-veg." In order for everyone to be able to eat, then, people had to be very careful never to do so. I do not remember learning these lessons, but particularly when I was small, before my sister and I were old enough to kick up a fuss, and perhaps also before my father had started to feel more at home with our neighbors than with other Indian immigrants, we went to a lot of functions. And my mother is clear that she taught me to be very careful about spoons.

I certainly remember that if we were grilling in our backyard, and vegetarian Indian guests were going to be present, my father would carefully and scrupulously scrub the grill beforehand and then make a fire, without cooking anything, to purify the grill. And then, if we were going to cook chicken on the grill, my father would do all the vegetable skewers before any chicken would touch the grill. My mother tells me that my father explained all of these rules to her, early in their marriage, and even then, they did not always manage to offer food that would work for their guests. She remembers one day when she had carefully made a vegetarian meal that would be complemented by naan, made on the grill. She realized that one of the guests, who did eat meat, had quietly warned his wife not to eat the bread because, cleaned and heated though it was, the grill had once been used to cook meat. The impurity of the grill could not be cleaned away, through scrubbing or fire, and the bread was irredeemably non-veg. (And, while I know the world I live in, and realize that I cannot get away with that level of purity, in the end, I actually agree with my mother's guest. I would never buy a used grill for my own personal use, precisely because one assumes that meat would have been, at some point, cooked on it, rendering it forever non-veg.)

All of these assumptions about how the world works, the unstated beliefs about what is done and not done, how to physically move through the world, and even what is natural and right turn out to be deeply culturally contextual. Their hows and whys are often explained by something called practice theory, advanced by a number of thinkers, one of whom is Pierre Bourdieu. A French social theorist during the second half of the twentieth century, Bourdieu was a public intellectual, equally claimed by the disciplines of sociology, anthropology, and philosophy. In *An Outline of the Theory of Practice,* he put forward his ideas about how culture works—what culture is, how it is transmitted. Part of what no doubt made Bourdieu so interested in theories of culture was that he had grown up in the South of France, the child of a postal worker and his wife, and became one of the premier sociologists and philosophers of his generation, mostly living and working in Paris. He was a man who moved between cultures in his own life and, perhaps, felt the strain of some of those moves. One of Bourdieu's key concepts is cultural capital—a term that has entered our lexicon, but often without the specificity that he initially gave it. Cultural capital is "the collection of symbolic elements such as skills, tastes, posture, clothing, mannerisms, material belongings, credentials, etc. that one acquires through being part of a particular social class."* When people share these things—a love of the symphony or of 1980s metal bands, a degree from a prestigious small liberal arts college, similar summer camps, or prep schools, or even accents, it creates a bond between them. Those bonds are why it can be so hard to do things like move between social classes or to new countries (or even different parts of the same country). It says something about you if you prefer Camembert to Cheez Whiz; if you went to a place that resembles the school in the *Dead Poets Society* or to the local high school with metal detectors on the door; if you know when to say "whom" or if you occasionally say "ain't."

Of course, what it says about you depends on who is doing the reading of the social cues. Was Barack Obama hopelessly elite for commenting on his love of arugula, or was that a sign

---

*"Habitus: Social Theory Rewired," http://routledgesoc.com/category/profile-tags/habitus, accessed December 1, 2018.

that he was, indeed, a Harvard man, despite being Black and the son of a single, if white, mother? More to the point, what does it mean that being "hopelessly elite" and being a "Harvard man" are exactly the same thing, the only difference being whether it is a negative or positive attribute? But though the lower classes are as skeptical of upper-class social capital as the upper class is of the capital of the lower, the cultural capital associated with the upper classes connects to power. Social capital, as it turns out, is as real as economic capital.

According to Bourdieu, cultural capital came in three forms: embodied, objectified, and institutionalized. Institutionalized is, perhaps, the most self-evident: credentials, degrees. Did you go to prep school? To an Ivy League university? To American schools or foreign ones? Objectified cultural capital is the most like economic capital, but it includes the signals that people send through how they choose to spend their money. What kind of car do you drive? Do you drive something super glitzy, like a BMW? Do you drive something solid, dependable, but either bought new or at an expensive price in the world of used cars, like a Honda or a Toyota? Or do you own something American, like a Ford? And was it bought used? Are you someone who could afford a BMW, and yet chose to drive a Prius instead? So, yes, objectified capital is about how much you can afford to spend, but it is also about how you choose to spend that money—do you wear very expensive clothing, but wear it until it is shabby, or do you always have the newest designer styles? Do you hunt for high-quality clothing at the Goodwill, because you know what marks something as high quality and classy and want to own those things without spending a lot of money—which breaks down the connection between class position and sheer economic buying power? Even the assumptions that structure my examples in this paragraph are based in the assumptions of cultural capital. The very concept of "classy" and the assumption that we all agree on what it means (we almost certainly don't) is rooted in our objectified capital.

Embodied capital is, perhaps, the hardest kind of capital to pin down—it is how you move through the world. What is your accent, but also, how do you modulate your voice? Do you make eye contact to show respect, or when talking to someone, do you show respect by looking at their chin, or at the ground, or anywhere but in their eyes? Bourdieu's term for embodied capital is habitus, and it is how, despite my coloring, Indians can pick me out as American (or at least Western) on the streets of New Delhi even when I am dressed in a sari, glittery sandals, and a gel manicure. These are unconscious but deeply ingrained behaviors—as becomes clear the instant you try to eat like a citizen of another country. Etiquette with knives and forks vary across countries, as do the rules for chopsticks. The rules for eating with your hands are different in India than in the United States.

Your habitus is all of these unconscious and embodied behaviors. Sometimes they are explicitly taught and other times they are not—someone probably taught you some aspects of how to use a knife and fork, others you probably just picked up from your environment. But one of the key things about habitus is that you do not know all the component parts of it, such that even if you wanted to tell someone exactly how to act, in order to blend into another culture, one that you knew very well, you would not be able to do it. Mostly because you would not be able to articulate all the little pieces of your culture—you simply are not aware of all the little things, and so they would be just slightly off.

Bourdieu contributes another important concept in understanding cultural capital—the idea of doxa, or the profoundly self-evident. Doxa is all our unconscious assumptions about how the world works, which makes all our cultural capital and cultural orientations seem self-evident. These are our deepest tastes, but also our deepest (and least considered) sense of what is "right." These assumptions are so deeply held that we think of them as universal, but in fact, they are deeply socially contextualized—not all cultures agree universally about what is or is not right or "natural." But those understandings of what is natural are so deeply culturally ingrained that they seem like instinct.

Essentially, it is why we, in Western society, can barely conceptualize eating dogs, but routinely eat pigs, which, as Jonathan Safran Foer points out, in his essay "Let Them Eat Dogs," is kind of nonsensical, given that dogs and pigs are of similar intelligence and social orientation. Our morality comes from doxa, but on a level that is so deeply rooted that it is pre-conscious and seems instinctual. Doxa is both created by our cultural capital and social location, and co-constituting with it.

A final relevant term from Bourdieu's theory of practice is dispositions, or all the unconscious and conscious aspects of culture that we carry with us. Dispositions include the things that you might consciously teach children (like, do not move the spoons from one dish to another, or whether or not one may belch at the table) and those that one might transmit or acquire unconsciously, like whether or not you greet the clerk in a store. For instance, saying nothing seemed totally natural to me, a New Englander, until the first time that I went to Alabama. There I realized that I was not sure whether or how to answer polite social questions about my health when I walked into a Southern grocery store. Do you say "Fine, thanks?" or "Fine, thanks, and you?" Do you break your stride as you say these things, or do you keep moving? No one teaches these things;

you just pick them up from the culture around you. They are made up of all the elements of your cultural positioning, from broad (are you from New York or Madrid or Vladivostok or New Delhi?) to narrower questions of your location within that culture (are you rich or poor, professional or working class, assembly-line worker or craftsperson, old money or nouveau riche, gentile poor or social climber?)

It is the combination of my deep disgust at meat—even fake meat, along with my own personal habits of not letting people use my dishes for meat, or bring meat to potlucks in my home—that make me think that perhaps aspects of my father's culture, of the habitus and doxa of a "twice-born" Hindu, plays into how I approach vegetarianism, even though the more I learn about Indian caste politics, the more that I wish it did not. The caste system is very complicated, and I do not understand all of its nuance, but at its most simple level, the twice-born castes are the high castes: Brahmins, the priestly caste, who were, according to the stories, born from the mouth of the god Brahma; Kshatriya, the warrior caste, born from his arms; and Vaishyas, the merchant caste, born from his thighs. The name "twice-born" refers to an initiation ceremony in which only these castes may participate, the sacred thread ceremony. Men receive a thread that they wear wrapped from left shoulder to right hip, and the ceremony is regarded as a second birth. While many high-caste people do, in fact, eat meat (many people living in India in my own Kshatriya, Panjabi, largely military family eat meat, and all my Indian relatives located in the United States, save one aunt by marriage, do as well), theoretically, high-caste Indians do not eat meat. As M. S. S. Pandian, a social scientist whose work focused, in part, on caste, noted, "It does not need much of an effort to understand what 'strictly vegetarian atmosphere' . . . encodes. It is caste by other means."

Vegetarianism becomes, then, a key way of marking some particularly vitriolic caste politics.

Part of being mixed means that I did not know that. I acquired the habits of a high-caste Indian, and particularly of a high-caste Indian woman, but I did not know the politics that those habits represented, even as the habits themselves seem completely natural.

Even if I am disgusted by the politics embedded in an aspect of Indian vegetarianism, I still carry with me both the disgust at the meat as part of my doxa, and the dispositions—sometimes internal logic, but often instinct—of how one makes one's choices. I will not eat a veggie melt from the grill at work because I can see it sitting there and cooking in the residual grease from the hamburger patty. And yet I wear leather. And yes, the leather that I wear is often bought used, particularly my leather jacket, but also the majority of my shoes. Here is the thing—theoretically, the leather should upset me every single bit as much as meat. While many American vegetarians do wear leather, many do not, and avoiding the two together is a modern American vegetarian disposition—I have at least one vegan friend who explains that she is disgusted by the idea of wearing leather. She knows that it is more durable and arguably better for the environment than the faux leather that she chooses instead, but it revolts her—just as the shared grill revolts me. But here is one of those places where, much to my surprise, one could argue that I have Hindu dispositions. Hinduism makes a distinction between what you put on your body and what you put in your body, and it is completely and totally acceptable to put leather on the outside of one's body, particularly on the feet—the most ritually impure part of the body.

And this is a mode of being in the world—attentive, however deliberately or unconsciously, to questions of purity or impurity that is at odds with the culture of my mom's Unitarian family, which values logic and rationality. For my maternal family, an explanation of vegetarianism that is rooted in animal rights or environmentalism makes sense, and would be honored, but only as long as it was logically consistent in a system of logic that was apparent to them. It makes logical sense for me to avoid meat in order to divest from a system that I find to be immoral, but not to avoid trace contamination that does not support the industry. That seems irrational. Of course, it is not so much that one system is rational and the other is not—it is that the systems are at odds and one is, for me, more a matter of instinct than of thought-out philosophical agreement. So, for instance, as far as I know, they have not actually put it together that I do not eat meat but do wear leather shoes (and occasionally will buy those shoes new). But if they did, I expect that the hypocrisy would be pointed out to me. But a question of purity or contamination does not strike them as rational and therefore would not go over well.

And so, in my own experience of my families, and my cultures, the question of what counts as rational thinking versus religious extremism, superstition, or unacceptable inflexibility strikes me as a deeply cultural thing. My Unitarian relatives, and their focus on a particular kind of post-Enlightenment brand of rationalism is, in the end, not outside culture—it is every bit as culturally rooted as the Calvinist sense of discipline that runs through my New England upbringing, or the Hindu notions of purity that cause me to shy away from soup that strikes me as contaminated. I tend to think that the conflicts that I experience in my family—on both sides—come from the fact that I hold pieces of both worldviews in my head. I am also forced to admit that I might not actually be correct about this.

And, in some ways, that is the weirdest thing about being a person of mixed heritage, and perhaps, even more so, of mixed heritage where half of your heritage is from an immigrant parent, such that you cannot (or do not) go and exist in their cultural world. It is hard to know precisely what forms your own doxa and where things come from. What seems like a clear-cut question of culture may turn out to be personality—after all, there are plenty of Indian Hindus, my own relatives included, who eat meat and plenty of Western vegetarians who wear leather and do not want their food cooked in a pan with meat.

For instance, while I am a Panjabi Kshatriya, or warrior caste, I have a friend who is a Maharashtrian Brahmin. If Panjabis are (stereotypically) known for being a boisterous and somewhat crude people, whose men, in particular, are likely to be hard-drinking meat eaters, even if they are high caste; Maharashtrians are famously abstemious. They are known to be vegetarians who do not drink. And these tropes go doubly for Brahmins. And these are the case in my friend's life. He is the person who explained to me why it is, in Hinduism, perfectly acceptable to wear leather on your feet, but not to eat meat. (Once again, while I do this myself, I did not realize that my instincts were likely rooted in what my Hindu family had modeled.) He rarely drinks, and only when wine or such is offered to him—he never even thinks to seek out alcohol. He has never, at any point in his life, eaten meat, and while he makes a mean cheese omelet, has a squeamishness about eggs that resembles my reaction to well-executed fake meat. And yet, he will bring meat into the house to be cooked in his pots and pans when his mother-in-law is visiting, whereas I have only twice even allowed meat to come into my house, as fully cooked take-out, to be eaten off paper plates. And he will eat vegetarian food from a grill where it sits beside meat. He identifies as a Hindu; he wears a sacred thread. But the inhibitions that structure my interactions with contamination do not operate in his life. He has, instead, carried forward a different set of those dispositions.

By the same token, while the inhibitions that structure my relationship to food do not structure the attitudes and approaches of all, or even most, of the Western vegetarians and vegans that I know (my friend Jacob, who is vegan except for bivalves, prefers to have his Impossible Burgers made on a grill next to meat because he then gets the flavor without the culpability), plenty do share my point of view. My friend Adrienne has spent years training her father to think of first her vegetarianism and now her veganism in terms of kashrut. It has taken a very long time, but he now grills her food with a layer of tinfoil protecting her food from the grill. My friend Thomas, neither vegetarian nor vegan, once brought a cooler of meat to an outdoor cookout at my house, because he was uninterested in the veggie burgers that he knew I would serve, but he also (without being asked) brought a separate grill and grilling implements, and then oversaw the operations to prevent cross-contamination. The fact that cross-contamination is a debate in non-Hindu or Buddhist circles has most recently become obvious in conversations about the Impossible Whopper and the fact that many vegetarians and vegans are concerned that the Impossible Whoppers will be grilled on the same grills as the regular Whoppers. So, clearly, this is an issue that matters to plenty of people who are not of Indian heritage.

And so, in the end, I will never know: do I have the sensibilities that I have because I have Indian heritage? If so, what do we make of the fact that I ended up with all the habits of a high-caste person without even understanding that those habits are ways of enforcing caste politics? Do I have them because

I am a particular brand of American lefty vegetarian? If so, what do we make of the fact that I do not have the same disgust for milk products that I do for meat, even though all my intellectual reasons for vegetarianism hold true for all animal products, or that I had been a vegetarian for twenty-five years before it occurred to me to worry about my leather shoes? This inability to know may be something that everyone experiences, but to me, it is fundamentally part of what it is to be mixed, and perhaps particularly to have an immigrant parent, someone raised with a different doxa than the one in which (in my case) he is raising children, who embodies another culture's habitus. I do not know where my doxa comes from, necessarily. And because of that, I do not know when my expectations and standards do not match those of my family and will cause us to unwittingly end up at odds with each other—as my aunt and I did about the ladles, in which the only thing that was clear to both of us was that the other had done wrong.

Three

FAILING THE AUTHENTICITY TEST

I cannot pronounce my own last name. I have known this for almost, if not quite, as long as I have known my last name. I can remember sitting with my aunt, years before she would marry and discard our shared last name, and her repeatedly making the consonant sound "ht," which we do not have in English. First she would make it on its own and then in the context of our name, and I would repeat it after her. I never quite got it right and beyond that, I could never quite hear the difference between what she was doing and what I was doing.

The Hindi alphabet, you see, has thirty-three consonants and between eleven and thirteen vowels, depending on which reckoning you are using. Each of those letters makes its own distinct sound. According to Before Their First Words, a project about human speech development out of the University of Barcelona, an infant can hear all the sounds that exist in human speech, which amounts to six hundred consonants and two hundred vowels. Between the ages of six to ten months, however, babies hone in on the sounds in their native language and not only lose the ability to focus on sounds that are not part of their native language, but also the ability to hear them. This is called perceptual narrowing or perceptual reorganization. Conveniently for me, the article produced by the Barcelona project that I am reading even uses the very letter that I am talking about. Its authors write, "For example, a child exposed to English loses the ability to tell the difference between different types of 't' sound (e.g., a dental /t/ and a retroflex /t/), whereas a child exposed to Hindi or Urdu would retain this ability as the differences in sounds are used to mark differences in meaning in those languages."

Presumably, a child raised in a truly bilingual home (my nephew's home, for instance, where one father speaks to him in Daddy's native English and the other in Papa's native Italian), would end up with the full complement of sounds. My home was not such a home. My father may have spoken to me, on occasion, in Hindi, Panjabi, or Urdu. Certainly, I know a collection of nouns. But at the time, theories of child development in the United States said that a child raised in two languages would never fully master either, and my father worked long hours and wanted to be able to speak to my mother and communicate successfully with us when he got home. And so we spoke English. Add that to an infant's innate preference for its mother's voice and inflection, and here we are: I cannot hear one of the two consonant sounds in my own last name.

Or rather, I can *almost* not hear it. I can tell when someone else is pronouncing my name "correctly." But I cannot quite pin down the sound. Sometimes, with great effort and several attempts, I can passably replicate the sound. I cannot, however, rattle it off naturally, the way one rattles off one's own name.

It is worth noting that many an Indian person, certainly my relatives (whether or not they share the name), but also various aunties and uncles whom I am only meeting for the first time, have felt free both in my childhood and in my adulthood to correct me on the pronunciation of my own name.

My name is a shibboleth, letting any member of the Indian community, or honestly, any non–South Asian person who has put serious time and effort into learning South Asian languages, know that I am, in the end, not authentic.

All I have to do, in order to fail the most basic authenticity test, is introduce myself. I have failed before I have even begun.

But what is authenticity? According to the *Oxford English Dictionary*, it is a term with shades of meaning, each of which plays out a bit differently in what it means, or could mean, to be "authentic," to Indianness, to one's self, given, of course, the possibility of authenticity at all. It might just be turtles, all the way down.

AUTHENTICITY:

1. The fact or quality of being true or in accordance with fact; veracity; correctness. Also accurate reflection of real life, verisimilitude.

Perhaps my biggest "failure" of authenticity, certainly my most longstanding, is that I do not like Indian food. As a small child, of course, I did not like most things. In the ways of little kids, I would take it into my head that I only ate plain pasta, with butter, or hot dogs. In that sense, the fact that, when my mother cooked Indian food at home or Boston uncles took us to Kabob and Curry for dinner, I ate only rice, dahee (yogurt), and roti (chapatis or, when I could get my hands on them, pooris) was more or less par for the course.

Once I was no longer a toddler, however, the fact that I did not like Indian food became a problem at community functions and family events. I heard about it endlessly, but there was nothing I could do about it. The food was simply too spicy and it all tasted rather overpoweringly of soap. I liked Indian food when cooked by my mother, who made milder versions and served the cilantro on the side, but I simply did not like fancy Indian food—the kind that inevitably showed up when other people were around. I tried eating around things, and was called out for it—we want you to feel comfortable, people would say while getting me special food, but also making a big deal of it.

This dynamic continued into adulthood, long after I had learned to eat things that I did not like in order to be polite and also after I had learned to be okay with, if extremely picky about, Indian food. It was, in fact, the central issue at the last meal that I voluntarily ate at my aunt's house. I had thought that my boyfriend and I were joining my aunt's family for a family dinner, just them and us. When we arrived, we discovered some sort of gathering beyond the immediate family. I do not now remember who the other people were—maybe extended cousins, maybe family friends of my aunt. Or, this being some combination of my aunt's way and the Indian way, people no one really knew, to whom we were being hospitable. They were not people that I knew, but they were people I suspected I might have to see again, and having expected something intimate, I was not thrilled to be mingling with strangers.

In her kitchen, to me, but also in front of the female guests, my aunt went on and on, extravagantly, about how she wanted me to feel welcome, and so even though she had cooked Indian food, she had made special vegetarian American food for me. Some days before the dinner, I had explained that she did not need to make special food for me. That I was an adult now, that I liked Indian food, and that even if I didn't, I would prefer to eat what everyone else was eating. She had ignored me. She wanted, she said, for me to feel comfortable in her home. I do not remember precisely what she made for me. In memory, it was a pasta dish, and, if I remember correctly, the deep irony of the situation was that I did not particularly care for it. Regardless, special effort had been made, and since I was tired and embarrassed about already having been marked out as "picky," I was determined to eat it.

Eventually, we sat down at the table, with my special American food, which I had tried to decline, and about which I was already uncomfortable—even my white, Jewish boyfriend was tucking into the Indian food—and my aunt started confiding to her guests how wonderful it was to have children who would eat anything. She admired that their children did eat everything and hoped that her children, my cousins, would do the same. I think she even said something about my pickiness, calling attention to my separate food. This was not the first time this had happened. It was not even the fiftieth.

In the context of meals like this one, feeling singled out means feeling identified as inauthentic. I realize that part of adulthood is that I do not have to show up at her house again. While my supposed problem was framed in terms of my pickiness, and not of my Indianness, it felt (fairly or unfairly) to me like my aunt was separating me out as not sufficiently Indian—likely because of my American mother. That interpretation was, of course, rooted in our relationship. In hindsight (and with Jhumpa Lahiri's fictional oeuvre under my belt), I realize that there are fears about immigration braided into this dynamic. But my aunt's conviction that I (raised in Connecticut) was too American, while her future children (who would be raised in Massachusetts) might be successfully Indian, had me convinced, from adolescence, that I was too American because of my mother—because of her genes or her influence, not because of where I grew up. I imagine it was reassuring for my aunt, to imagine that my mother, her genetics or her culture, was the reason that I was not Indian enough, such that she, her genetics or culture, could be the backstop, something to hold off the overwhelming influence of American culture on her own children.

As an adult, I eventually learned to like Indian food in restaurants, though I continue to be a bit annoyed when it does not match my expectations—restaurants often use tomatoes when my family would not. This may or may not be "authentic" for another region of India than my family's—the one where the restaurant owner is from, for instance, but I only go out for Indian food out of a desire for the comforts of home. I have also developed more of an ability to eat spicy food, though I have never become someone who likes really hot food. When I lived in Philadelphia, I ate out a lot with someone who adds hot sauce to his food and eventually, every time he got up to get it, or requested it from a waiter, we grinned at each other over my incomprehension of his ways. On a short trip to Boston, a best friend once ordered me a second dinner when the one we were sharing caused my eyes to water in pain. Perhaps, I thought, my inauthenticity is not that I do not like Indian food. Perhaps it is that I cannot handle heat.

During this same period of my life, I made friends with a couple, both of whom are half-Indian and eat Indian food at home all the time. And I ate at their house frequently. I liked the food at their house. It was never too spicy for me. At some point, I observed that I was surprised by this, and they told me that this is a standard practice in India, to make kid food (either for the kids or for the entire family) that is milder than the standard adult food, and then to ramp up the heat as the kids get older. I sat there and stared at them over the mild and kid-friendly Indian meal, as I realized that, throughout my childhood, I liked most of the Indian food served in my house, where it was milder. The take from the extended family was that our food was "mild" because it was made by my American mother. The mild food of our household was considered, despite my mom's status in the family as an excellent cook, insufficiently Indian. This, however, makes no sense. My mom was, in my childhood, the kind of person who got into jalapeno-eating contests in friends' gardens, and my Indian father was someone whose digestion was disrupted by hot food, regardless of how much he enjoyed eating it. But more to the point, it began to occur to me that my parents had been doing something deeply traditional, serving kid food, which my childless aunts and uncles did not want to be bothered to do. But because my Indian father struggled digestively with spicy food, in our house, no one "turned up the heat" as the children got older.

By the time my aunt had small children of her own, the fact that I would have separate food was already established, and so I do not know if my cousins were exposed to hotter and hotter food only slowly, over time. I do know that I was considered inauthentic because I did not like hot Indian food, when in fact, the expectation, in actual India, for actual small children, is not that they will like adult food. They are trained and taught to like adult food. I was caught in a double bind—judged as inauthentic by the same people who were not, actually, giving me an authentic upbringing.

Up until this point, I have been talking about authenticity as if it means exactly what the first definition from the Oxford English Dictionary suggests—being true or in accordance with fact. Can I be truly Indian if I cannot pronounce my own name or if spicy food makes my eyes water or if cilantro tastes like soap to me? Or is it simply that without these measures, others will not perceive me as Indian? What if I learned to pronounce my name, perhaps never quite perfectly, but in the way of many white Sanskrit scholars, who work hard, practice, and can articulate a version of the sound? What if I got COVID-19, lost my sense of taste, and could all of a sudden eat chilies and cilantro without turning a hair? Would I somehow become more authentically Indian? Or is it possible that "true," "in accordance with fact," or "authentic," at least when applied to human identities, are a chimera? Is authenticity even possible?

Authenticity is, functionally, about identity. And identity, as philosopher and critical theorist Judith Butler tells us, is about regulation. "Identity categories tend to be instruments of regulatory regimes, whether as normalizing categories of oppressive structures or as the rallying points for a liberatory contestation of that very oppression," Butler writes in the essay "Imitation and Gender Insubordination." As you can see in the title, Butler is talking about gender, which they argue is more about what one does than about who one is—"what one does" signals behavior, otherwise known as gender performativity, whereas "who one is" denotes an essential or innate way of being. Women, as anyone who has ever tried to walk in high heels realizes, are not somehow naturally inclined to teetering in heels. We wear high heels for any number of reasons, but largely because of what they signal to us and to others about the kind of woman we want to be or to be taken for. This applies, according to Butler, not only to aspects of gender that are clearly choices—some days I wear heels, and sometimes I wear ballerina flats, and sometimes I wear Doc Martens with yellow stitching—and to aspects that feel like preferences—why I have long hair, for instance. It also applies to things that do not feel like choices at all—how we pitch our voices or move our bodies—but that, research has shown, actually do depend on cultural contexts. Butler argues that all of this is gender performativity, even if not all of it is conscious.

Gender is not the only aspect of identity that is performed. When I do not like Indian food, when I profess that I do not like Indian food (because it draws a laugh), when I locate that dislike in my disappointment that it is *not as good as my mom's*, or when I say it is because I cannot take the heat, I am performing an identity, and changing the identity through my performance. When my half-Chinese friend asks the waiter at the Chinese restaurant for chopsticks, he is performing an identity of Chineseness for the waiter. When he comments to me that he was doing it to assert an identity that he felt the waiter was ignoring when he did not offer them, he is underscoring his, and our, shared halfness for me. The idea that these identities are performed does not mean that they never feel quite right— sometimes they do. But they regulate our identity. They ask: Are you performing your identity as Indian or Indian American correctly? And do you have the right to perform it that way? And if I decide instead to highlight my lack of enthusiasm for Indian food, or my lack of tolerance for heat (though, if we are being honest, I also hate the excessive sweetness of many Indian desserts soaked in simple syrup), I am performing my failure of Indianness, sometimes consciously and explicitly because I want to assert my Americanness, sometimes because I am annoyed because I feel like people are assuming that I would prefer Indian food, and sometimes because I do not want to go out and consume a meal that I suspect that I will not enjoy. Sometimes I perform these preferences as a failure—I do not like Indian food—and sometimes I do it to assert a claim to Indianness—Indian restaurant food disappoints me because it is not home-cooked food. If I claim not to like Indian food and neglect to mention that I like my mom's Indian food, that I like Indian food with the cilantro removed, and that I like most South Indian food, well, I am pushing against some-one's definition of what appropriate Indian identity might look like—just like I am pushing against the confines of my straight, cis-gendered womanhood when I stop shaving my legs. But in both cases something is being regulated—I understand how to perform the identity and I understand how to not perform it. Neither of these positions, Indian or not-Indian, lipstick femi-nist or bra-burner, exists in total freedom. And, of course, even the idea that identity is performed, and performed for an audi-ence (even if you are the only audience), deflates the whole idea of authenticity a bit. It certainly deflates the idea of a core and "true" self that might match the performed self.

Of course, if you are half and half, your performance is al-ways subject to critique—by people who are vested in which identity you perform; in how you perform both identities; or in demonstrating that, whatever you have chosen, you are not doing it well enough. For instance, in Hindi, every kind of aunt or uncle you might have comes with a specific title. So, father's brother is Chacha; father's brother's wife is Chachi. Mother's brother is Mamaji, and mother's brother's wife is Mamiji. The suffix "ji" means respect and can be slapped onto any other form of address, ranging from a given or last name to a profession, and I cannot tell you why, in my family, we use the title of re-spect for one set of aunts and uncles and not the other, though I actually suspect it is to avoid confusion with the English words Mama and Mommy. In addition to these uncle-based terms, father's sister is Bua and mother's sister is Masi. There are words for their husbands as well, though in my family, we call them all Jijaji, which is a polite word for "brother-in-law." It basically means "my sister's honored husband." There is a less polite word for brother-in-law that works in the other direction—the word you would use for your wife's brothers. No one will teach me that word, because, at least according to my mother, it is used as a vulgarity to imply "I screw your sister." In my father's generation, there were at least three words in play for older brothers, with which one you used depending on how close you were to each other and where in the birth order you fell, a special term for their wives, and at least two terms for older sisters. I know them all. I use them all. I just wrote this paragraph for you off the top of my head, which is why it does not include the terms for uncles by marriage, which we tend not to use.

Now, there are also terms for father's brother and his wife if the brother is elder to your father, Tayaji and Tayiji, respectively. Because I am the daughter of the second son, I originally thought that the term was only for the eldest brother, but apparently, it is for all older brothers. Regardless, that term and its companion is what I should, theoretically, have called my father's older brother and his wife. When my uncle came to visit, when I was a toddler, I may even have used those terms—certainly, I have always known them. But at some point late in elementary school, my aunt came to visit. I called her Tayiji, and she explained that she wanted to be called Chachi. Being called Tayiji made her feel old. Fine. Done deal. I call her Chachi, her daughters call my mother Chachi. It is all egalitarian and "authentic," in so much as no one is using the (equally commonly used in India, but for parents' friends) English word "auntie."

Fast-forward more than a decade. I am twenty-four years old, in my Chacha and Chachi's living room in New Delhi, at a function associated with my cousin's wedding. For some reason, I need my aunt's attention. I address her as Chachi. After she has moved on to the next guest, her brother-in-law (my cousin's uncle, but not mine), who lives in the United States, and knows my parents, and knows that my mother is not Indian, says to me, "You know, really, you should call her Tayiji." This is what I mean when I say that sometimes it is annoying—sometimes deeply and profoundly annoying—to fail the authenticity test. I do not think that this particular mansplaining windbag would have corrected me if I were fully Indian, though perhaps he would have. (He is the kind of person who expected his relatives call him Doctor Sahib.) His correction assumed that my family could not teach me what they wanted to be called, that somehow I did not know, that it was his place to correct. But it also triggered in me a hot flash of shame. How could he think that I did not know how to address my own relatives?

2. The fact or quality of being authoritative or duly authorized; authority. Now rare.

While the behavior of a stuffed shirt of a relative's relative is, perhaps, trivial, not being (or not being perceived as) an authority has other challenges as well, in part because it can undermine your ability to shape your engagement with a culture in which you are expected to participate. Because I am not only American raised, but half-white, I am presumed to be an outsider, without the authority to critique Indian culture. This plays out in two different ways.

First, as the daughter in an Indian family, I have experienced any number of gendered expectations about how I will live my life. Are you (as an American objecting to whatever is being dished out to you) a Western feminist imperialist who is disrespecting a culture, or are you a daughter in/of that culture who, by right of having it imposed upon you, also have the right to object to its patriarchal, misogynist fuckery? What if your Indian patriarch is the person who pointed out its patriarchal fuckery in the first place? Why do you, old Indian man who is some sort of cousin, get to impose your culture on me?

I do not want to pretend that it is easy for Indian feminists to push against the patriarchal aspects of Indian culture, and when they do, I imagine that they are open to the accusation that they are being disrespectful of Indian culture, they face the possibility of being told that they are too Western. But for me, with my Indianness in constant play and question, such an accusation heads me off at the pass. Because I am mixed, I do not know how to be Indian, and because I am indisputably partially of European descent, the implication is that it is an act of imperialism for me to criticize Indian ways of being and familial patterns. That said, because I am also a daughter of the family, I am held accountable to them.

Of course, in an immigrant context, or a mixed heritage context, the question of authenticity is also in constant play. The "authentic" India that my father and his siblings and the friends in their immigrant cohort left behind is not the India that exists now. This means that whenever I write about my experience in terms of gender (or any number of other aspects of Indian society), I am not referencing the India that exists now—I am referencing the India that my father and his friends and family remember from the 1960s and 1970s. As a historian of (among other things) gender in the United States over the exact same time period, I know that gender does not function in our society now as it did in the 1960s. Of course, the same holds true for India, but not necessarily in the imagination of immigrants, particularly immigrants of that generation when traveling back and forth was expensive and often rare. It is also, of course, an India of memory and imagination—more dramatically drawn than the real place. It is always either the filthy and backward place that was escaped or the longed for utopic home to which one wants to return. It is rarely a multi-faceted place.

And, of course, in any moment, there are always multiple Indias. Think about it—there are at least four Americas right now: the America of the Black, the brown, the Indigenous; the America of their actively anti-racist white allies who are doing the work to avoid being in the next category; that of nice white people, who are well meaning yet damaging, not hateful, and who hurt at the idea that they are racist; and the America of my neighbors down the street, whose gigantic, hand-painted Trump 2020 signs stayed up past the attempted coup in January 2021. So too there are multiple Indias now, and multiple Indias in the moment frozen in time by any given person's act of immigration.

The reality, then, is that there is no stable India that one can depict. As a result, one cannot meet, for instance, the standards of the older generation—the immigrant generation that shaped my childhood, and the standards of my immigrant and ex-pat colleagues, who came to the US more recently and who travel back and forth more frequently.

And here is the final way in which the authority issue is interesting/a problem. Sometimes, when I meet, for instance, Indian academic ex-pats—colleagues who grew up in India but have academic careers and sometimes academic training in the US or Canada—I have noticed that the bits of culture that make me feel most Indian, most connected to Indianness, most "authentic," are often things that these people do not share. Two parts of my life come immediately to mind: Divali and vegetarianism.*

---

*Divali is more commonly spelled Diwali. The second consonant, like the one in my last name, is a sound we do not quite have in English and is between a *v* and a *w*. The *v* spelling that I have used represents the spelling that I grew up with, and the trend in my family (and my own) pronunciation.

One of my Indian-born colleagues talks about Divali having a deeply problematic racial underpinning, and possibly also racially problematic implementation. They had lots of Facebook posts on the topic as the holiday rolled around. The Facebook posts, however, were predicated on a shared understanding—from the posts alone, I could not quite figure out what the issue was. The Facebook posts, however, did mean that when I joined another desi colleague for happy hour drinks, I was not surprised when she made similar comments. She made these comments in passing and did me the honor of acting like I knew what the hell she was talking about. I liked that feeling and did not want to reveal my ignorance, and so, in that moment, I did not ask her to explain. Before I could ask her in another setting, COVID-19 closed school and stripped hallway conversations and after-work drinks from my work life, and so the casual moment never presented itself. But between that and the Facebook posts, I know there is something here that I do not understand.

Maybe it is algorithms, but when I look up Divali and racism, I do not find descriptions of Divali as being racist and problematic. I find descriptions of racist attacks on Hindus celebrating Divali in the US, Canada, and the UK. This is not the racism I mean. I want to know why an internal Indian conversation would find Divali to be racist. Eventually, I realize that while color is one of the topics in play, perhaps I should have been searching for information about caste. By that time, however, I had already emailed my second cousin once removed to ask. While I suspect I would love her answer, I never heard back, and I realize exactly what had happened—I asked a big question that requires thought, time, and attention. My email is now in her list of things to do "when she has time." And as we all know, that time never really comes. Instead, I find myself imagining what my colleague might have meant. In my imagination, when my colleague says that she has all sorts of complicated feelings about Divali, I think about my own response to Thanksgiving.

I love Thanksgiving.

My father was in retail—the Christmas season was his busiest time of year, and Thanksgiving was a whole day of Daddy time, in the middle of the prep for the season and the actual season. There were aunts and uncles. Eventually, there were cousins. We made special food. The next day, we got to have pie for breakfast. I watched, every year, a happy cartoon about mice who came to the new world on the Mayflower. The mice had a courtship that largely mirrored Longfellow's "The Courtship of Miles Standish." And then I grew up and became a professional historian of American religion. I use words like "settler colonialism" in my classroom on the regular, if not every day. And yet, I still celebrate Thanksgiving. I am uncomfortable about it. I cannot always get home, but when I can, I spend the holiday with a close friend who describes her own commitment to the celebration as her "most egregious ritual practice." But I do celebrate it. I would be miserably depressed if I spent the fourth Thursday in November doing business as normal.

And so, when I imagine my colleague's complicated feelings about Divali, I imagine my own complicated feelings about Thanksgiving—the political awareness, the warm family memories, the complicated and not-warm family memories, and questions about how my lefty friends think about it when I appear in my dear friend's shots of her Thanksgiving table.

I imagine all of these feelings for my colleague, but they are not my feelings. And I do not even know what the ugly underside of Divali in myth or practice might be.

I tell my friend Briallen all of this and she tells me: you need to go and figure this out. You need to read up on Divali, you need to figure out what is at stake. My reaction to Briallen's advice is to check in with the colleague across the hall. This involves, of course, admitting to her that I had no idea what she was talking about, and such an admission is possible for me precisely because of two experiences that I have had with her, one during that conversation in the tapas bar, and one since.

Here is what she said and did that disarmed my fears of inauthenticity. As we were sitting with our white American colleague, senior and a mentor to me and a cohort-mate and close friend to her, the colleague across the hall noted that she is aware that people raised in the diaspora feel very differently about Divali than she does. She did not say it with the suggestion that these experiences were less valid or less authentic, just that they were different. Her tone of voice, and the arc of her comments, suggested that she finds these differences interesting, and valid.

And here is the other reason: in the run-up to the 2020 election, our department chair and my colleague arranged a panel of Black, Indian, and biracial women reflecting on then-vice-presidential candidate Kamala Harris. Since there were three panelists, one of whom identifies as Black, and one of whom seems to identify as Black and biracial, I was, perhaps, the Indian presence, though it is possible that our moderators, Black and Indian themselves, felt that those three terms would cover the multitude of identities that the five of us had between us. In the preparation for the panel, and during the panel, my colleague from across the hall listened to my thoughts on Kamala Harris and identity—I explained, for example, that while I hear the criticism that Harris is comfortable with policing because she is from a Brahmin family, and, in India, the police prop up Brahmanical supremacy in the same way that, in the US, they prop up white supremacy. While I am not suggesting that such takes are wrong, as a mixed race person who grew up on the edges of Indian culture in the US (as I suspect Harris did), I do not really understand caste. I rarely comment on it, because I do not know much about it. I am not sure if I do not understand the caste system because I grew up in a diasporic Indian community in which shared language and culture trumped caste, such that it was "post-caste," or because I grew up in a diasporic Indian community whose ability to be in the diaspora was so tied to caste and privilege that it was actually made up almost entirely of people with "caste privilege." In other words, was caste invisible not because people were beyond such things, but because everyone was the same? I suspect the latter, and I suspect that, for Harris, like for me, my family's caste location structures everything about what I think it means to be Indian. But I certainly do not know enough about caste to offer a critique of it, and I do not know which of my assumptions are, in fact, tied to caste. The colleague across the hall listened to these thoughts, validated them, and both seemed to understand my claim that I do not really know anything about caste while gently pointing out that everything about how I, for instance, enact my vegetarianism is caste-based behavior.

But she did not use that opinion to argue that I *do* know about caste, but rather to see my point: your behavior can be shaped by forces that you do not understand, but that does not mean that you know about them or that they are consciously important to you. And she also did not judge my experience— she did not imply that I should, for instance, understand caste better than I do, or that my failure to understand is tied to shame or a failure to have appropriate pride in being Indian.

And so, finally, I ask my colleague what she meant about the problematic racial underpinnings of Divali. She explains that part of why I do not know about these cultural objections to Divali is that they are relatively new, and she also helpfully sends me two or three articles to help me understand. I read them. As explorations of the Ramayana, they are interesting. That said, I do not have enough in the way of context to connect these articles to the cultural shift currently underway. They are filled with terms that I do not know, and cannot parse through basic Google searches.

And so, I try again. Nandini, a friend and former neighbor, a political scientist focusing on feminism, politics, and social movements in South Asia, posts an article on Facebook and muses, "Trying to figure out if Diwali is worth celebrating as a fun festival that connects our children of the Indian diaspora to the homeland, or if it's another Brahmanical celebration of caste oppression. Is there a way to celebrate and still critique?" Another mutual friend poo-poos her concerns, saying that, in any celebration, there will be things that are disgusting and things to celebrate, and that basically, she should not be a killjoy. Nandini clarifies her question in her post. Is Divali like Thanksgiving, a holiday that has complicated politics and problematic mythologies, but one that can perhaps be re-caste (pun intended, and mine, not hers), or is it more like Columbus Day, a holiday that should be wiped out, or completely replaced with some other reason for a long weekend in October? I am thrilled! In her framing, Nandini has validated my metaphor.

Though I do not know her well, I like her a lot, and I decide that perhaps she is the person to help me tease things out. Besides, it seems totally fair to assume that a woman with a full teaching load, a research agenda, and three children, two of whom are now remote learning through a pandemic, will have the time and energy to help me explain my heritage. I ask her about the article. She sends me a link to the article in English. I read it and, once again, simply do not know enough of the terms to understand what is in play. Once again, I impose on Nandini. Over the phone, she explains that one piece of Hindu mythology argues that gods and asuras, which she translates as demons, are half-brothers and were originally equals, but in the beginning of time, they battled, and the gods used trickery to win the battle. Thus, they became more powerful, and became the writers of history. Today, there are Dalit writers who assert that they are the asuras—that the higher castes are the gods, who have oppressed them not because they are better but because they have controlled the narratives (and most other forms of capital) and written the history to facilitate the oppression of Dalits. The Ramayana, the central text of Divali, then, is problematic because it is the celebration of the victory of a god, Ram, over the demon Ravenn.*

Is there, I ask her, a myth that says that the Dalits come from the asuras? She says that the argument is that it is a pre-Vedic story, and so there are not texts, but that is the Dalit assertion. She points out that there are plenty of other reasons to object to the Ramayana beyond this complaint. There are, she

---

*Once again, the spelling that I am using here deviates from the standard. The *a* that can appear at the ends of these words is functionally an inflection on the final consonant, rather than a full *a*. While the pronunciation is perhaps best described as between, for instance, the English words "Ann" and "Anna," I grew up saying something much closer to "Ann" than to "Anna." By contrast, some words actually do end with a real, rather than an implied, "a." Those words are usually feminine, and the contrast is more like the names Paul and Paula in English. So, while we often spell the hero of the Ramayan "Rama," his name is pronounced much more akin to Ram, while one of my mother's dearest friends is named Rama, the "a" is pronounced, and the name is feminine. In terms of the Divali story, then, I grew up reciting a story of "Ram and Sita," rather than "Rama and Sita."

says, other places where caste shows up problematically in the text otherwise and (and this was totally obvious to me, even as a child) the text is problematic from a feminist standpoint for any number of reasons. There are, essentially, a collection of solid political reasons that one might cancel the holiday. But, as Nandini pointed out, the holiday is more that its politically problematic elements—it is a celebration of Lakshmi; it is a harvest festival; it is a time for street theatre, and families and special food. Nandini has not decided whether this is a holiday to cancel, or one to, as Loretta Ross puts it, call in, but she has helped me to understand the dilemma. She has also, like my colleague across the hall, but unlike at least 75 percent of my family, managed to do it without shaming me. I feel mastery.

First and foremost, like feminist objections, her explanation raises the question: am I, as a foreigner, as someone who does not actually understand the caste system particularly well, allowed to offer such a critique of Indian culture? And if I am not allowed to offer criticism, does that mean I am also not allowed to participate in revisioning a holiday that I love? If I am also, perhaps, not someone with the authenticity, the authority, to innovate—if my innovations are inauthentic, am I then participating in politically objectional behavior? If I cannot innovate or critique, and do not want to participate in caste-based oppression, do I need to forego the holiday? And if I forego the holiday, am I even more inauthentic: a mixed race ABCD who does not even know or respect my heritage enough to maintain a major holiday?

But, if my authenticity is in question, if I am not Indian enough, do I have the cultural authority to enter this conversation at all, either to critique or defend? Here are two other questions about Divali and me. Given everything I now know about the complicated politics of Divali, and given my imagined comparison to Thanksgiving, I am fairly certain that if I were raised in India, and maybe if I were US raised by two Hindu, Indian parents, I would share my colleagues and friends' discomfort about the holiday. But for me, Divali is one of the pieces of being Indian of which I feel the most uncomplicated ownership and joy. It is a holiday that we always celebrated at home, under the control of my parents. It was a big deal—we had guests, and usually my sister and I could each invite a friend. There was a big dinner, there were homemade Indian breads and desserts. We wore fancy Indian clothing that had the same excitement of our Easter dresses, which were worn for Easter Sunday and then for music recitals, and then, in the fall, when they were almost outgrown, for regular church. Because we spent the holiday at home, my parents called the shots—the story of Divali was tailored to our feminist, Unitarian home. My parents replaced the Lakshmi puja with a Sarasvati puja, because they believe that education and music are more important than wealth—a family value that has not necessarily worked out well for us—my mother because she comes from generations of Protestants who valued living simply over a Weberian sense that money was evidence of virtue, and my father because he argued that the lesson of Partition is that no one could take education from you. My father would one day tell my sister and me that one chants "om" because it helps people connect to the concept that Quakers call the Inner Light. We got out the Christmas lights and put them on the rubber tree plant. The children received presents. The visiting friends got presents. There were candles. I feel so much ownership of the holiday that I have celebrated it in my own home, sometimes making Hinduism grad students help me with pronunciation, but never even worried that my way might be wrong. I *own* that holiday, and while I worry that it makes me a terrible person, and I worry about celebrating it in my new location, with the colleagues who made me aware of its political implications, it will also have to be pried from my cold, dead hands. (I miss living near my friend Susannah, who is the kind of competent person that sizes up your family traditions, learns them, and helps you create them every year, with neither any sense of being a tourist nor a sense that she somehow has taken over your thing.)

3a. With reference to a document, artifact, artwork, etc.: the fact or quality of being authentic; genuineness.

This is the kind of authenticity that comes up when you are sightseeing in India. All the main tourist attractions, the ones owned by the government, have two prices listed: the one for Indians and the one for foreigners. There are, I believe, two logics to the price difference. First, Indian tax dollars are supporting the public park/forte/ancient astrological instruments/Taj Mahal, and so it seems fair that Indians would pay less. Also, the logic goes, the average foreigner who might go traveling around has considerably more disposable income that the average Indian day tripper or local resident, and likely has an exchange rate working in their favor. Why not make them pay more?

Theoretically, the issue at hand is one of citizenship. The Indian government is thinking about taxes and potential revenue, but in practice, the ticket-wallas, the guys charging admission rates, are not checking government-issued IDs to decide who gets what rate. They are reading their customers. And they are using any number of characteristics.

My friend Allia talks about how, when she and her sister traveled in India, what they refer to as their ambiguous ethnicity was written on their bodies. The Dhody sisters, who are half-Indian, one-quarter-Cuban, and one-quarter-white Anglo-Saxon Protestant, are very fair. Allia has what you might call a "wheatish" complexion, particularly when she is tan (as she usually is when in India). A wheatish complexion is, perhaps, the color of lightly toasted bread. It is a good thing, in a very color-conscious Indian society. If it weren't coupled with Allia's sarcastic and insubordinate personality (Allia is from Philly, where booing is a constitutionally protected right), she would have been a hot commodity on marriage websites like shaadi.com. By comparison, my skin is probably more the color of very strong Indian-style chai—the underpinning tones of tea, but as dark as a Starbucks latte. Anna, Allia's older sister, however, goes beyond wheatish skin. As their Bua, their father's sister, put it when looking at the color coding on shaadi.com, "Anna is just off the charts. Anna is so fair that there isn't even a term for her." Note that this would be good, if it did not throw Anna's Indianness into question. And so, when the Dhody sisters stepped up to pay their entrance fees, Allia was routinely charged the local rate and Anna the foreigner rate. Anna failed the authenticity test: she was obviously mixed, impossible as an Indian. The one time Allia got caught, the giveaway was that she was wearing short shorts. "No Indian girl," the ticket-walla said, "would wear shorts like that." When I got caught, it was more in the way that Allia got caught. I do not wear short shorts, but there were Doc Martens peeking out from under my salwar chemise; also, I thought I could register opinions with my father, as if we were adults traveling together rather than a man traveling with his unmarried daughter; and when I registered those opinions, I did so in English.

When I was in India with my father, the two-tiered price system drove him completely nuts—he basically found it inhospitable. One should, he argued, be a good host by not charging guests a higher rate. I was equally annoyed by his annoyance: we could afford the higher rate, and given that, it seemed churlish to pay notably less than I would pay to go to a museum at home. I suspect that what really upset him was that he hated being told that he was not Indian, though he had given up his Indian citizenship the first chance he had. When we were buying tickets, therefore, my father would want me to stand back and not talk, to not do anything to give us away as Americans. One day, when the ticket-walla charged us the foreigner price, my father reprimanded me for having spoken. The ticket-walla came to my defense: sir, look at yourself. My father, in his baseball cap, Birkenstocks, Yale t-shirt, and blue jeans, had read as American, language notwithstanding. I was deeply satisfied by my father's failure to pass: this was an instance in which my authenticity was not, entirely, tied to my mixedness. After all, my father, who was so Indian that he was born in the British Raj, could also fail the test.

I found my father's failure to pass because of American cultural predilections satisfying, largely because they were the same tendencies that often undercut my own claim to Indianness. I grew up in the 1980s, in what was essentially the first generation of Indian immigrants to have and raise families in the United States. In 1965, Lyndon Johnson signed new immigration laws that made largish-scale immigration from Asia to the United States possible, at least for highly skilled professional people. So, for instance, though my father worked in a store, when I was a kid, the operating assumption was that my father was a doctor or an engineer. My father trained in law, which is, in the end, a less portable and transferable skill, and though he thought of himself as a businessman, he worked for a store called Bradlees, which was the 1980s precursor to big-box stores like Target. Right there, we failed an authenticity test— my father's immigration story was not quite right. Outside the Indian community, this means that I cannot answer questions according to the expected script. My father was not a doctor, was not an engineer. I am from suburban New Haven, but we are not Yale people. Inside the Indian community, our class status created a different kind of authenticity problem, particularly among my fellow ABCDs, all striving to establish their own credibility. No, I did not go back to India once a year, once every other year, several times during childhood. I had never been. And with that, I lacked the stories; the tourist experiences; the relationships with aunts, uncles, and cousins; the fledgling language skills; a sense of the smells, tastes, and sights of another country and any sense of another world in which it might have been home.

But the thing was that these were high-caste, high-class people who were in the United States for a better life but were not necessarily enthusiastic about becoming American (not that immigrants ever necessarily are). There were ways in which life in the United States was a step down, but even when it was not, many of the adults in these communities had a lot of anxieties about whether their children would be Indian or American. They were afraid of the potential difference that can arise when parents and children are separated by culture and afraid that their children would be too American. America meant dating and disrespect for elders and questionable education and bland food and wide-open spaces.

This question haunted the adults in my family, long before they even had children. I remember my aunt confiding in me that, even though she knew that American ways of showing respect were not inherently bad, it would make her very upset if her children showed respect in American ways instead of Indian ways. I do not remember what I had done, but I remember another hot and this time bitter flush of shame. If I were my aunt's daughter, she would be disappointed in me.

In this way I was an object lesson for my aunt: a high-achieving and loved but nonetheless unacceptable child. My sister and I served as the human embodiment of those fears for the Indian immigrant community with whom we would sometimes hang out. One of the primary ways in which we exemplified these fears was through language. We would go to parties in suburban homes throughout the New York metropolitan area, parties that required driving up along the Hudson, or over the Whitestone Bridge to Long Island, or the Tappan Zee into North Jersey. The parties can't possibly all have been in ranch homes with finished basements or in rented halls with folding tables and chairs, though that is how I remember them. The women would be in the kitchen or in the family room, wearing floaty saris during the day, or heavy silk ones, stiff with embroidery, at night. The men would sit in other rooms, and play cards and drink, or talk. It was always too hot, perhaps because of the crowds or perhaps because the heat was cranked for the party, so that women could wear their saris in comfort. Maybe these friends always kept their houses hot—why move somewhere for a more comfortable life that involves central heating if you do not actually use the central heating? (By contrast, I grew up in the kind of flinty, descended-from-Calvinists household where we keep the thermostat below 65°F in winter and turned it down at night.) I usually did not like the food. I did not like all the people speaking in languages that I did not know. I did not understand these strange houses without dogs or cats. All of this made me feel odd and out of sorts, like I did not belong. And I was constantly making small mistakes: I never called the strange adults auntie or uncle, which marked me as different.

In the end, though, it was not the small mistakes that I made when I was among the adults that I remember it most—it was what happened when we went downstairs, to the Lord of the

Flies setting that was the children's parties. The parents some-times found the shared bond of Indianness enough, whether or not they would have found themselves to have anything in common in India itself. But just as Jhumpa Lahiri writes in *The Namesake*, the kids at these parties see each other, if not every weekend, many more weekends than they want. We did not go to these parties every weekend the way that the other kids did, and therefore we were outsiders. Overtly, the outsiderness was not about being mixed: I suspect that, if we had been reg-ulars, we would have become insiders. But, of course, we were not regulars because we were mixed. My mother was happy to spend some time in immigrant communities, and had friends there, but she also wanted to spend time with people whose experiences were more like hers—we belonged to a church, and so had competing weekend commitments and communities. And the very fact that my father would marry out also indi-cated that he wanted a life and a community that went beyond the weekly gatherings of the immigrant community. So, our mixedness was not the overt reason for our exclusion, but it was central to it.

Because kids are kids, they did not necessarily want to have to play with the strangers, and as it turned out, they had the perfect way to exclude us: language. Because my mother, the native-English-speaking parent, was our primary caregiver, English was the language that we spoke at home. Neither my sister nor I was conversant in Hindi. We could not speak, we could not understand, other than sometimes, getting the gist of a conversation. It was therefore enough to switch languages for the other children to exclude us. They never got in trouble for deliberately excluding us by switching to Hindi or Panjabi, and if you think about it, this too makes sense. They were children of immigrants, and, if my cousins and Mandarin-speaking high school friends are anything to go by, they probably re-sisted speaking the parental language and preferred to speak English. Part of why their parents brought them into these South Asian spaces was to get them to speak Hindi or Panjabi. Whether or not the parents were going to put it that way, they were not going to undermine their own agenda in order to help the half-breed kids to feel included.

And here is the thing—this is a complicated reality. Their desire to have their kids speak Hindi (or Panjabi or Urdu) was not unreasonable. I often wonder what it was like for my father not to have a shared language with his immediate family and have read, in studies of Asian American families, about how a language barrier between parents and children can result in culture being lost. Also, given that we were, at best, dropping into a community, it makes sense that this community would not worry too much about what we needed—we would only appear a couple of times a year. While, in retrospect, I sort of blame the parents of those children at the parties for not mak-ing their children make us feel more welcome, I understand their language impulse.

But at the same time, that dynamic set up a reinforcing circle. I do not feel welcome and accepted in Indian spaces, especially around my peers. I do not feel welcome specifically because I do not have the skills, the markers of the identity. As a result, I did not, for instance, want to join the Indian students' group when I got to college. (This was partly because, ironically, they wanted to speak Marathi. India has a lot of lan-guages. Even if I spoke one of my family's languages, I would not have spoken Marathi.) I did not want to join because I felt like I would be judged and found wanting. But then, my failure to join, like my inability to speak my last name, became proof positive that I did not belong.

3b. The quality of truthful correspondence between inner feelings and their outward expression; unaffectedness, sincerity.

I think of this definition as the kind of authenticity that is summed up by the comment that Polonius makes to Laertes in *Hamlet*: "This above all: to thine own self be true. And it must follow, as the night the day/Thou canst not then be false to any man." To the contemporary reader, this phrase essentially means that you should live according to your core values. When one hears this quote in its inspirational context, it is supposed to mean that, if you live in accordance with your internal truths and values, you will live a good life, in which you treat other people well or consistently, and move through the world as you should.

This understanding of how to be in the world might have made sense to the modern self, in a world where people assume that a sort of core self exists and can be accurately depicted and reflected. But we live in a postmodern age, and we do not have this understanding of the self at all. The postmodern self is a fragmented self, based not so much on the idea that there is "no there there" as on the concept that there are many selves. The question of which self might come forward is always a question. And it becomes a fraught question when the question of which self, which identity one puts forward, is political (or politicized).

It is interesting to note that the inspirational reading of the quote is likely not what it meant to the Shakespearean reader— Polonius, who is not a moral exemplar in the play, was likely telling his son that one is a better person in human relations if one is operating from a place of financial security, and that therefore, he should put his own self-interest first. And since Polonius is not a sympathetic character, I am not sure if he is even supposed to believe that putting yourself first ultimately allows you to be a better person, or if he is just justifying bad

behavior. When I asked my friend Brantley, an English professor who regularly teaches Shakespeare—though he would
want me to note that he is a Chaucerian, not a Shakespeare
scholar—if I had gotten Polonius right, he wrote back, "Since
it seems the point is that there *is* no one true self, then using
a quotation from a suspect character is an effective way to do
that. I'm of the school that all Polonius's advice is meant to
seem either insincere, empty, or self-serving."

Shakespeare's understanding of the self is complex, and it
allows for layers and possibilities of human identity, affect,
self-understanding, and self-beyond-what-one-can-understand.
What it does not allow for is a true self, an authentic self, a self
that could pass or fail an authenticity test set by many forms of
identity or diversity politics. Shakespeare's self, or lack thereof,
suggests that the concept of authenticity might be a chimera,
because we have many selves. And it is this reality, that of our
many selves alongside the gatekeeping and litmus testing of
identity politics, that posed me so many problems in my for-
mative years.

I do not want, when I am in Indian spaces, to worry that, if
I am me—with my American senses and sensibilities—then I
am somehow not performing an adequately Indian identity. I do
not want my family to be frustrated because their own choices—
about immigration, about marrying an American (on my father's
part), about not spending her twenties hanging out in subur-
bia with her brother's young children (on my aunt's part)—have
shaped me to be less Indian than they would have liked. Their
choices were not necessarily bad. I am glad, after all, that my
father immigrated and married my mother. I am sympathetic to
his desire to bring siblings here and to their desire to come. I also
understand why my aunt wanted to spend her twenties being
young in Philadelphia, rather than hanging out with toddler me.

But those choices created a me that is more comfortable with ballet than Bharatanatyam. I am comfortable with that me, but I do not want to be judged for it. Similarly, I do not want to be judged when in non-familial spaces, when not being Indian enough is read in terms of a rejection of culture, or in terms of assimilation to dominant norms. The challenge here, however, is that while there is certainly performativity in play, for me, there is also the complicated intertwining of upbringing. I am not "acting white" because it gets me more power—I am acting white because I was raised by a white woman. There are lots of ways that one could then criticize that behavior, either for its foolishness (the cultural capital of whiteness, and non-immigrant status, is something that I have; the skin privilege of whiteness is not) or for the inherent problems of white culture. But then I should be criticized for imbibing the values of a white supremacist culture, just as anyone else raised in such a culture should. I should not be criticized for "acting white," as if I am discarding my brown heritage in an attempt to pass. I am not posing when I prefer matzo ball soup to khichari—one is my childhood comfort food and the other is not. And that preference has more to do with the gender politics of who cooked in my childhood home than it does with a desire to obscure Indianness.

But for me, there is this sense that if I were me, if I stopped code switching to fit into the cultural space that I am in and just sort of presented myself as I am most comfortable (which yes, according to Butler is still based in performativity, but also feels the most like "me"), then somehow I would automatically fail. There is an expectation that I will be more Indian than I am. Mixedness, however, the idea that I might contain multitudes, does not quite fit into anyone's boxes and does not quite work.

Four

AMERICAN RACISM

About a year ago, I saw an unattributed comment on Instagram that I keep thinking about. It parsed the experience of the children of non-white immigrants: your parents sacrificed a lot to come to the United States to give you a better life. They worked and struggled. They gave up a home in a place where they spoke the language easily, understood the culture, had a network, had a childhood, had extended families. Immigrant parents do not want to hear that, in doing so, they turn you into a racialized minority. They want to have come to America to give you a better life. They want it to be an unambiguously better life, in order to justify all that sacrifice. This can mean that they are stunningly unwilling to hear about experiences of racism in their children's lives and/or to interpret events in terms of racism, even though they may have had experiences of racism themselves.

White parents of non-white children can also be very resistant to thinking about racism in their children's lives. After the killing of six Asian women in a 2021 shooting spree that left eight dead and caused a national (and surprisingly long) reckoning with anti-Asian violence, many Asian American children adopted into white families wrote extensively about what it is like to be Asian, trying to talk about race with white parents. As Nicole Chung, a transracial adoptee, wrote in *Time* magazine in its March 22, 2021, issue,

> Yet I've found myself wondering: If my adoptive parents were alive, witnessing the spike in anti-Asian racism and violence in the U.S. and around the world—with Asian women the most common targets—would they be concerned about me? Would they understand why I cried when I told my own Korean American daughters about the spa shootings? Would I have reached out to them during this past hard, heavy week, or held back, uncertain of how to share my fear and rage as the only Asian in my white family?

Chung notes that her parents loved her and would have done anything in their power for her, yet they struggled to see her as Korean American. She says that they did not talk to her about anti-Asian racism. They did not discuss model minority myths, being seen as a perpetual foreigner, or exoticization. She says that it was not that her parents thought that she was white, or that their whiteness did not extend to her. It was that, because they were white, they did not think about race at all. They saw race—theirs, hers—as irrelevant, and from the position of their white privilege, assumed that since they did not care about her race, no one else would either. Chung's is the most prominent piece that came out of that moment, in terms of Asian adoptees with white parents, but her comments echo through lots of writing from such adoptees.

I am not the adopted child of white parents. I am not the child of two immigrants. I am the biological child of one South Asian immigrant parent and one white American parent. You might think that such a combination would provide the skills for living in the United States, preventing the cultural gap that can exist between immigrant parents and their US-born kids, while also giving the child a parent who has the experience of life as a minority. One of them could help me with being Indian and the other with being American.

But I have come to wonder whether that combination created parents who were uniquely poorly suited to prepare their children for American race relations. In this case, by unique I do not mean "particularly bad at it," as I realize that many immigrant parents resist the idea that their children may be more American than they would like, and that many transracial adoptive parents are stunningly bad at thinking about that racial difference. Rather, I mean that my parents were particularly set up to think that they had their bases covered, when in fact they did not, even if they fully realized that the experiences of the mixed race Indian American kids they were raising would be very different from their own.

Unfortunately, my parents, if they thought through what it was going to mean to have mixed race kids (rather than thinking that they loved each other and wanted children), did not quite anticipate what it would mean to be brown in America. My mother has said that they thought that the world was changing, and they thought that the United States would grow into a truly multicultural society—she is, in retrospect, disappointed in how little progress the world has made.

But beyond their idealism, neither of them really had the skills that go into being a person of color in the United States. One of them grew up as a high-caste person from a racial and religious majority, and if his family was displaced and not wealthy, they were nevertheless in the middle class. He certainly believed that he was coming to the United States for a better life, and he (as so many immigrants do) assumed that a better life would come from hard work and education.

My mother is white, with all the liberal politics that would lead her to have much to say about racism in the United States, and all the best intentions in the world. That said, it is hard to know what you don't know, and she sometimes fails to understand how white privilege works and also has lots of assumptions about American racism structured by a Black-white binary. Maybe most importantly, as she learned about being a person of color in the United States, she learned through her relationship with my father and from the community of immigrants that she belonged to because of him. Because she was his wife, and because she experienced both discrimination and embrace within the Indian community, and because she experienced sexism, both in the community and in her marriage, the lines of power were not always clear. She did not necessarily experience white privilege within the context of her marriage—from the outside, it looked like she experienced a complicated blend of sexism and support.

My father needed to believe that his experiences were about immigration more than they were about race. We talked about racism in my childhood, but there was not a lot of space for the idea that it might happen to us, that we might need tools for its navigation. It was something that happened out in the world, to other people (principally, Black people), and we had an obligation to be part of their fight. And because often the racism that we experienced did not match the racism that we learned about, and because it was not identified as such, it was hard to learn that it actually was racism.

There are two family stories, from the early years of my parents' marriage, that I think it would be fair to call stories of racism. The first is pretty simple. My parents were trying to buy their first house. My father worked long hours, often on weekends, and so my mother had more time to look for a house than he did. She therefore did a lot of looking at houses, and the plan was that they would look together at any houses that she had liked. Only, over and over again, when they would go back together, mysteriously, there would be far fewer houses to see. More than ten years later, when they sold their first house and bought the house that my mother still lives in, the experience was jarring enough that they went back to the only real estate agent who had not discriminated against them and hired her to be their selling agent. Our pediatrician's wife was a real estate agent where we were moving, and trusting her (and also trusting someone Jewish to know about housing discrimination and to avoid it), my parents worked with her to find a new house.

Despite their care in finding a real estate agent who would treat them well in our move to our new town, my parents also framed the move, from a working-class community to an upper-middle-class community as, in part, a way to get away from racism. In the new town, people would be more educated. We were moving largely for the public schools, but also for a different kind of community, one that would be more sophisticated, more cosmopolitan, and with less bias. My parents' attitudes are familiar: they held the idea that it is the lower economic classes, the people whose manufacturing jobs have dried up, the people without power, who are the engine of American racism. They assumed that an urbane, sophisticated space would not be racist—that no one with a Yale degree would drive a pickup truck with Confederate flags. Of course, racism did exist in the new community—it just looked different. The Yale campus may not be covered in overt Confederate memorabilia, but that does not mean that it does not police non-white bodies in the name of "community safety," or memorialize slavery in its stained glass. Until 2017, it had a residential college named for John C. Calhoun, a white supremacist and passionate defender of slavery. And if we are talking about money, rather than education, it would (of course) be a fundamental miscalculation to assume that country clubs or the Daughters of the American Revolution were at the forefront of integration efforts. But while intellectual and cultural sophistication and wealth did not equal an absence of racism, it is true that the bias that did exist functioned underground and was harder to see. Of course, in some ways, as the other family story of racism shows, it would not take much for the other community to appear to be less racist.

The second story that I am about to tell is a combination of childhood memory and adult research. In my memory, I was pretty young, and there are reasons why, as you will see, it would make sense to think I was about eight, that these events thus happened in or after 1986. But I feel younger than that in my memory.

When I was little, and my father worked for a New England department store, he fired someone for shoplifting. This happened periodically, and always upset my dad, or at least did when he liked the employee in question. He would be upset at dinner and then it would be over. But after this particular firing, the phone calls started. People (or a person) would call my mother, ask for her by name, ask if my father was Black, accuse her of miscegenation. They would tell her that they were waiting in the parking lot for my father to close the store, that they would kill him. They would describe my father's car, a blue-gray Datsun sedan with two doors and a stick shift. They would recite the license plate number. They identified themselves as the KKK. Nothing happened when my mother called the police. Sometimes, my father would receive threatening phone calls, either at our house or on nights when he worked late and was the one closing the store. (For years, I had the idea that once, when my mother called the police, she thought she recognized the desk sergeant's voice as the voice from the phone calls. When I asked her about this, as I wrote this essay, she responded, "I only had that experience once. Daddy thought he had it many times." It may or may not, of course, be true that the voices were the same. Perhaps, tired of what seemed like inaction, my parents came to imagine it to be so. Perhaps the inaction was because the voices were the same. I will never know.)

When the voice called on Christmas Eve, my aunt was at our house. My aunt is a lawyer. She told my mother to call the FBI. The FBI told my mother that they would investigate, and that they would call the local police as a courtesy. The calls stopped, but we never heard much more about it. This is why my family suspects the police were connected to the phone calls, either directly or through a social network (as in, the police were not making the phone calls, but were somehow connected to the people who were, or were simply in sympathy with them). Of course, it is possible that the FBI was simply able to root out the problem or that, with the support of the FBI, the local police were able to root out the problem, and for some reason, no one ever followed up with our family. In childhood, I came to understand that we had been targeted because my father had fired a Klansman and the KKK was seeking revenge, and as a mixed race couple, my parents made an easy target.

Just as there is no way to know whether my parents were correct when they connected the police to the Klan, there is no way to know whether the calls actually came from a Klansman, or simply from someone trying to create and evoke the terror of the Ku Klux Klan. Anyone can pick up the phone and create terror. You do not need to be a Klansman to create terror in a mixed race family, and to paraphrase journalist Adam Serwer, the terror is the point.

That said, here are the things that I do know:

In 1986, the *New York Times* wrote an article about James Farrands, titled "The Catholic Connecticut Yankee Who Heads the Klan." He was the Ku Klux Klan's first Northern Grand Wizard in 120 years and he lived in Shelton, Connecticut, which is where my family lived in the 1980s. According to Farrands, as quoted in the *New York Times*, wherever the Grand Wizard lives is the headquarters of the KKK. So, while I was living there, my (original) hometown happened to be the headquarters of the KKK. (Note: Farrands was also the first Catholic to head the Klan, which began admitting Catholics during the Kennedy administration.) The same article reported that, according to the police, around five hundred members of the Klan existed nationally, and about fifteen members lived in Connecticut, most of whom were in Farrands's family. In 2016, an article by historian Christopher Perilla in the *Hartford Courant* noted that fifteen was also the FBI estimate for Connecticut Klan members.

While the Connecticut estimates were low, nationally, the Klan was alive and well in the 1980s. For instance, in 1985, Glenn Miller, founder of the Carolina Knights of the Ku Klux Klan, had, according to the Southern Poverty Law Center's Klanwatch Project, twenty-three local units and one thousand members. Miller's group was drawing from surrounding states, but I found these numbers helpful, in preventing me from doubting my memory because I was tying the Klan too tightly, in my mind, to the 1920s. I also find myself wondering, why, in the mid-1980s, the police claimed that the national number of Klan members was almost exactly half the number that the Southern Poverty Law Center recorded in a North Carolina–based group alone, according to a Klanwatch Project report. While I do not know the reasons, two possibilities present themselves. The first option is that the two groups have different systems of counting, and because of the racist origins of American policing and criminal codes, the police are structurally set up to undercount membership in or affinity for such groups. My second thought, and one that feels compelling given the events of my lifetime, ranging from the beating of Rodney King to the deaths of Trayvon Martin, George Floyd, and Sandra Bland to the story of Kyle Rittenhouse's interactions with the police, is that white supremacy is baked not only into systems but into sympathies, and that such sympathies lead to undercounting. Whether my inclinations are correct or not, the fact remains that, at least in the mid-'80s, the police and a group dedicated to monitoring hate groups dramatically disagreed about how strong such groups were.

Though I grew up knowing the story of the suddenly shrunken housing inventory, we did not talk about what that experience of racism had meant to my parents or what it might mean and how it might play out in my life. And while I have memories of the experience with the Klan, and perhaps we discussed it at the time, I do not remember talking about it very much. Certainly, I do not remember conversations about what racism might look like in my life, or whether it might touch me.

This does not mean that we did not talk about racism at all. We talked about police racism, but it was always framed as anti-Black racism. This take on the situation could have been because of Asian immigrant (or Asian American) faith in the concept of the "model minority." There are many flavors of model minority myth, and all of them are harmful, both to the people who hold them, and to their ability to be good intersectional allies to other minorities. The flavor of model minority that I know best is the Hindu South Asian version. Journalist and novelist Sanjena Sethian described it this way in *Time* magazine: "Indian Americans from my subculture— usually wealthy, dominant-caste Hindus—often actively embrace stories casting ourselves as America's great successes, as the outsiders who confirm the meritocratic American dream." In this formulation, racism will not hurt Indian Americans because, in essence, we do not deserve it. It is a problematic view, in part because, when the racism inevitably comes to Indian Americans, people who hold this view can only respond in one of two ways: to deny the racism occurred at all or to blame the victim, for somehow not working hard enough, not being enough of a "model" minority, or for not walking the correct line between being "too American" and "not American enough." One's status and right to avoid discrimination are not based on a fundamental sense of human dignity, but rather on a particular mode of performance—and therefore the status is always precarious. Of course, an important other reason that the model minority myth is problematic is that in order to be a model minority, someone else has to be the "not-model" minority—in this logic, then, those people deserve whatever racism comes their way.

To an extent I actually think my parents' reticence rested on a different foundation: my father, as an immigrant, even a non-white immigrant, and my mother, as a white American, even a liberal one who believed racism existed, were simply unequipped to teach their children about American racism.

My father seemed to understand the discrimination that he faced as professional frustrations derived merely from a lack of network. When he tried to break into the American business world—a world he seems to have navigated smoothly when he lived in India—he struggled. He explained his difficulties as a problem of not knowing the right people: as an immigrant, he did not have the alumni networks that connect people—no Ivy League undergraduate networks, no Wharton MBA. All this was true, of course; those networks are real, and as an immigrant who had not received his education in the United States, my father was barred from them, whereas he did enjoy their equivalents in India.

Left unmentioned in these conversations, however, were the ways in which gender, race, and class play into these networks. In our family narrative, the assumption was that if my sister and I worked hard and applied ourselves, we could obtain the networks that my father lacked. We were Americans; what was the issue? And because my mother is an American whose father enlisted in World War II after his freshman year at Harvard, and because Harvard counts the Harvard men who went to World War II as alumni, whether or not they ever returned to its hallowed halls, we were legacies. I had claim to Harvard legacy status. We were Americans. We would succeed. We would achieve the dream.

My father loved America with a passion for all he believed it could be, but part of that love meant believing that his adopted country was a place where people were judged "not on the color of your skin but on the content of your character." If Martin Luther King was articulating a dream, my father needed to believe that he lived in a version of the United States in which that dream was actualized.

On the white side of my family was an unspoken assumption that racism is only the big things—the police beating Rodney King on the news or kneeling on George Floyd's neck. If you disapprove of that racism, if you march against it, or buy (and maybe even read) the books that the independent bookstores put in their windows about racial justice, then you cannot possibly be racist. Even more so, if you call the resulting unrest "protests" rather than "riots"; if you bemoan that people are more concerned with loss of property than with loss of life, with generations who have seen their dreams deferred until they sag like a heavy load and then, perhaps, explode; and particularly if you know whom I just referenced, you cannot possibly do things that are racist. And additionally, actions taken by other well-meaning liberal or progressive people cannot possibly be racist. Certainly, what this means is that if a well-meaning liberal or progressive person loves someone across a racial line, as my white family loves me, it is hard for them to see that our interactions are, at least at times, shaped by that racial line and its power dynamics. It is hard for them to see, and therefore was hard for me to learn to see, and to name, that these interactions, with people who loved me, who were invested in me, were also shaped by systemic racism.

It is hard to know what to do when the racism is present in your private space, your home, your family.

I am deliberately drawing a distinction between the actions that people take and their essences—we all do racist things, we are all implicated and shaped, in our unconscious, by the systems that govern our society. My goal here is not to demonize people, but to parse out the harm that the inability to see racism does to people of color in white families, and to see what racism does to the relationships, valued by both people of color and their white families. In the same way that I would argue, as a feminist, that patriarchy hurts men, not as much as it hurts women and nonbinary people, but in real and substantial ways, unexamined systemic racism hurts white people, perhaps particularly those who want to be in loving relationship with people of color.

Sometimes, perhaps, the racism is even a result of their own desire for closeness. This is the kindest way that I can understand an interaction I had with my aunt while I was in college. I was living with her for the summer, so that I could have a job in the big city, rather than in my town, so clearly she supported me. She was, after all, housing and feeding me for the summer. I came downstairs dressed for the day in a salwar kameez, the Indian traditional dress that is flowy drawstring trousers and a top, which, depending on the style of the moment, might range from tunic length to a dress, knee length or longer. I do not remember what had prompted this fashion choice, or even where I was going—work? Out with a friend? Nowhere, because it was the weekend? I might have chosen the outfit because it was new—had my father's sister just come back from India with a gift or two? Was it particularly hot? It was an unairconditioned New England summer, and a cotton salwar kameez would have been nice and cool. Maybe I was experimenting with wearing Indian clothing more. Maybe I had shifted into wearing Indian clothing a decent amount at college and so I did not particularly think about it, one way or the other. Whatever the case, I came into the kitchen for breakfast and my aunt looked at me and said, "What? So you are super-ethnic now?" She said this twenty-five years ago, and I can still remember her tone of voice, which was somewhere between disapproving and cutting. And I also remember the flush of shame that I felt at my choice of clothing.

I am not sure why I felt shame, though I recognize that this time, with my white family, it was for doing something Indian, rather than not being Indian enough. Was it because I was wearing Indian clothing and that was unacceptable, or did I feel the shame because I felt like a poseur, like I did not have the right to the Indian clothing?

This is not a kind of racism that we ever talked about when I was a kid. I could talk, with my mother, about the ways that my father's family and the Indian community made me feel not Indian enough, but I could not necessarily talk to her about what happened in the context of my white, liberal, Unitarian Universalist family when I experimented with being Indian. That was left to me to figure out, and to sort out. And part of what was challenging about that was, by and large, my mother's family was the place where I felt like I belonged. And so it was the place where these moments were the most shocking and painful.

But also, what, precisely would have been the problem with being super ethnic? What might my aunt's objection have been?

One way of understanding my aunt's comment is that she is a racist jerk who was inappropriately policing my failures of whiteness—that we cannot do anything about the color of my skin, but we can WASP up my behavior, or other aspects of my being, in a way worthy of the Daughters of the American Revolution. But I really do not think that was it. For one thing, my aunt has never shown the slightest interest in the DAR.

Another option is that my aunt wanted to protect me from racism, from failing to assimilate. I had not experienced this kind of racism yet, but now, as an adult, I most certainly have. During the 2016 election, I was spit on in the grocery store and on the subway (though usually while wearing jeans, or a dress). Perhaps my aunt saw that possibility coming and wanted to head it off. This was definitely what was going on when she barred me from going to certain neighborhoods in the city, where she believed racial tensions would be high, and where she thought I would be at risk. (She protected me in other ways as well—when I went with a friend to an Indigo Girls concert that summer, she insisted on meeting the friend, on talking to her parents.)

I suspect it was partly that. But here is what I suspect was the biggest piece.

I think that we want our families to be like us. That we do not think that we should have to navigate the politics and power dynamics of cultural difference in our intimate family spaces, and that we want our children, whom we love and mentor, to be like us. To have them not be like us feels like rejection. To have them *announce* that they are not like us can feel even worse. (I deduce this from my mom's reaction to my announcement that I was converting to Judaism. No one could have been more supportive of the decision or of the life than she was, but she did skip a beat at the announcement when she clearly felt hurt and as though she and her values had been rejected.) While they do not write books on how to be a good aunt, any parenting book will tell you that this project of self-replication is a fool's errand. But it is a natural desire, and cultural compliance is a low-hanging fruit. (And also, again, one might be used to navigating difference and having to be culturally sensitive in public, but not in one's own kitchen.) I think my aunt saw a foreigner in her kitchen when she wanted and expected to see her sister's child. I think the disconnect was jarring, and I think my aunt spoke out of that disconnect, and because she is white, she did not think about the fact that the generational power dynamic was not the only power dynamic in play.

Meanwhile, I was actually paying my aunt a compliment—I was showing how much I trusted her—when I decided (consciously or unconsciously—I no longer remember which) that I did not need to code switch while in her house. I was signaling to her that I felt at home. If you read articles about code switching, many of them talk about, for instance, the ways in which minorities change their language or behavior in the workplace. These articles talk both about the advantages people get when they code switch well, and about the cost of doing so—a typical elementary school example would be the child of immigrants who decides to buy school lunch or begs for a peanut butter sandwich so that their classmates will not see them eating whatever food their family traditionally eats, even though they love the taste of their mother's cooking. The code switching elementary school student avoids getting teased for "weird," "smelly," or "gross" food. On the other hand, they may experience shame or embarrassment about their family's food, be worried that they will experience that shame when a friend comes over to play. (I remember the discovery that, even though we ate Indian food no more than once or twice a week at the very most, friends thought my childhood home smelled different. This fact was, in fact, confirmed by one of my American aunts, who underscored that she loved the way the house smelled, and since she did always want my mom to make Indian food for her, in retrospect, our house was always extra fragrant when she was around.) Even if they are not experiencing shame around their food, if they have decided that they need Lunchables in order to fit in, rather than say, a turkey sandwich and carrot sticks, the act of code switching can simply land a kid with a lunch that is arguably neither as healthy nor as appetizing as what would have come from home.

For minority people who are not mixed, be they people of color, immigrants, religious minorities, or a combination of those things, their families' circles are places where they do not have to code switch (unless it is, in fact, code switching to go from the dominant culture into the culture of the home). Code switching is often exhausting—for some people, it comes very naturally, and there are those who argue that it is a more natural skill for people of mixed heritage, but it is relaxing to be in a space where you do not have to do so. And so, for many, the family, or community, becomes a sanctuary.

Despite the fact that my family had multiple races and cultures in place, the idea that I could be culturally myself in my home was largely true for me growing up, at least as far as my nuclear family went. We had a family culture that drew from the overlaps between my parents' cultures of origin, and from the things that they liked best about their own or each other's cultures and wanted to continue. Sometimes this looked like basic things: we ate a mixture of Indian, American, and fusion food. We celebrated a range of holidays represented by the religions and cultures in play. There was a strong focus on education, a shared cultural value. My sister and I took music lessons and were allowed to go to small liberal arts colleges, representing my mother's side of the family. Our home was always open to visitors, a value that was certainly from my father, though whether it was an Indian value or more of an immigrant thing, I cannot say. As I have written elsewhere, and as my cousin suggested when I asked what struck him as Indian about our house, we dealt with food in ways that drew more from Hindu norms than Unitarian ones.

Outside of the nuclear family, however, I had always code switched, or at least tried to do so. My decision not to do so around my aunt was actually a sign of my comfort with her, but it was a mistake—she disapproved. And I again, I think (or thought) that she disapproved because it made me somehow other.

Of course, a few years later, I would proudly show her a horribly ugly, but deeply voluminous apron that I had found at the American Friends Service Committee's annual clothing sale. It was (and still is) both hideous and sort of fabulous in its hideousness. Her comment? "Well, it certainly isn't slimming." So maybe she is just, on some level, lacking a filter. But (and here is the thing), while she also made me feel temporarily lousy about some combination of my body and my apron, her bluntness about the apron did not cut in quite the same way that her bluntness about my Indian clothing did. And this is part of what is tricky—I think, were I ever to talk to my aunt about these two comments, she would not see them as different. She would have her reason for speaking out—a desire to have me look a certain way, a failure to filter. And she would not understand, or be able to see, that the difference between the Indian clothing and the ugly apron mattered to me. And it certainly shaped my sense of whether or not it was okay to decide that I did not want to code switch, but rather to present a blend of identities. Now, basically, I code switch.

Is the kind of comment that my aunt made racism? My mother says that when she was raising her small children, she did not know the term code switching, but she thought a lot about how a behavior that worked with our father's family might be misunderstood and chastised in her family and vice versa, and she worried about how much that might hurt. She worried that it would be shocking, painful, and confusing to be rebuked for behaving in a way that we were confident was correct, and to receive that rebuke in family space. When she and I talk about my aunt, reacting to my donning of Indian clothing, she commented that she thought her sister saw me as "taking on an identity," something that she might have found annoying and performative, particularly as a white American liberal baby boomer who had seen plenty of people appropriate Indianness. And so she rebuked me for performing an identity, rather than expressing an identity that I already had, or experimenting with an identity that I had a right to. In my best guess, she was not meaning to "make me act white." She had forgotten that she and I had a different relationship to Indianness.

So, is it racist?

This story is not actually different from the stories of not being Indian enough for my Indian family, and yet, while I do not raise the specter of racism there, I do raise it here. And that is because racism is, more than anything else, about power. Outside of a family, criticizing an Indian or an Indian American person for wearing traditional Indian dress would, indeed, be racist.

But if your standard for racism is violence or the kind of structural disempowerment that affirmative action is supposed to combat, if there is no space in a discourse of racism for talking about microaggressions, it becomes hard to both name something like what happened with my aunt as a form of racism, and to talk to her about it, as something that is more than just an aunt attempting to bring up a niece, as she sees fit and as is her right.

It is not, however, just that microaggressions are hard to see and hard to articulate, and that my white mother did not have the tools to talk to us about those things; it is that many white American cultures are deeply silencing.

My mother comes from a midwestern WASP culture that tends to minimize. This is an ethos of personal responsibility, stiff upper lips, and making do. But this is not only a culture of the upper Midwest or of white Anglo-Saxon Protestants. It is alive and well where I grew up in New England, as well—my friend Karen (who often comments, "My name is Karen but I try not to *be* a Karen," and it is in her comment that she tries rather than an assurance that she succeeds that she demonstrates how very much she is *not* a Karen) is a New England Jew, and she says that growing up, any time she came home from school with tales of someone being mean to her, her mother would respond, "Well, what did you do?" My college best friend talks about how Southern manners dictate that you make the other person comfortable, and so he has dismissed people's apologies when they have made heteronormative assumptions about him, rather than thanking them for the apology. In his corner of the United States, you minimize the harm done, for the comfort of the person who inflicted the harm.

My friend Kate, midwestern and Catholic, rather than WASP, points out that in addition to a stiff upper lip, there is in these circles a cultural aversion to whining. And indeed, whining is, in my book, one of the worst things one can do. Let us be clear, we have cultural examples from earlier eras in white American history that take the stiff-upper-lip and an aversion to complaining to the extreme. At the beginning of *These Happy Golden Years*, Laura Ingalls Wilder writes about going away from home to teach school for the first time. She boards with a local family—the Brewsters. The home is unhappy. Mrs. Brewster cannot cook, makes no attempt to be cheerful or even to dress. Laura, trying to manage, stays cheerful, offers to help with work, and tries to make small talk. Eventually she gives up, and in her giving up, her judgment on Mrs. Brewster (and her sympathy for Mr. Brewster) is palpable. Laura shows Mrs. Brewster no sympathy for her potential misery, just judgment for the misery that she brings on others—which is maybe fair, but also does not ask what her experience might have been. But more striking than the lack of concern for what might have been Mrs. Brewster's depression and desperation is Laura's pride that she never reveals the strain of her living conditions to her parents. The school is a challenge, and she does seek out her mother's advice—Mrs. Ingalls is a former schoolteacher herself—and she is proud when the advice works, but she never says anything about her living situation. Even when Laura, then just fifteen years old, wakes up one morning to realize that, outside of her curtained bedroom, Mrs. Brewster has pulled a knife on Mr. Brewster, demanding to go back east, she still does not tell her parents. She is proud of not complaining, and of managing the situation without putting anyone out. When her parents reveal that they knew it was difficult and are proud of her, she objects that she did not complain, and her forbearance becomes another reason for their pride in her. Years later, when she recounts this story, Laura the author doesn't comment on it, and the virtues she still upholds in her narrative perfectly exemplify the stiff upper lip—she finds a sense of strength and value in enduring abuse cheerfully, not in advocating to not be abused.

A milder, and more contemporary, version of this cultural sensibility can be seen in Dar Williams's most famous song, "Iowa," when she sings about a culture where one does not inflict one's passions on other people, where one avoids being a bother.

There is, of course, a significant difference between not meaning to be a bother and being a fifteen-year-old who does not mention a knife-wielding landlady to your parents, but I would argue that they still represent points on a continuum of the same cultural value. Management of one's struggles—and the repression of unruly or unpleasant emotions—is a value.

And to be clear, this is a culture that judges a failure to keep a stiff upper lip. In adulthood, I have talked to my mother about this. She came from a family in which complaining, whining, could bring on painful disapproval or even more serious conflict. In training her children not to complain, she was trying to protect us from painful experiences with family, and with other people from that stiff-upper-lip culture.

Like any other cultural value, this one is complicated. Yes, things are more pleasant when everyone makes the best of difficult situations, especially if the difficult situations cannot be helped. Whining *is* really annoying if you are in the car for a ten-hour drive with someone who complains about the drive, but there is nothing to be done about the situation. Pointing out sexism or racism—such as always having to do the photocopying or make the coffee, fielding sexual advances at work or comments about your accent, receiving requests to touch your hair, or being constantly told, overtly or subtly, that your cultural approach is inappropriate—calling out those things, however, should *not* be seen as whining; this is something that the culture of managing and not whining can miss entirely. But language shapes understanding—while the term microaggressions was coined in the 1970s, my mother says that was not a word that she knew, and without the word, the concept was elusive. She says that once she knew the word, much later, once I was an adult, it was easier to see microaggressions—the racial ones in my life, the gendered ones in both of our lives.

But this is an essay about mixedness, and if you come, in part, from that very white American culture of not complaining, it can make it harder to see, address, and figure out how to talk about microaggressions. And it can make it hard to explain these moments to your family, hard to obtain or even request their support, because they, who do not experience the same things, will hear your complaints as minor.

In part, this means that, instead of having the support of your family when you talk about microaggressions out in the world, your family may gaslight you, as they try to bring you up or shape you into a person who inhabits their values of meeting adversity with a stiff upper lip. Because they are conditioned to think of racism in terms of big issues—like violence in policing, redlining, and racial profiling by the TSA, and because microaggressions are often so small as to be invisible to the white viewer, when you try to articulate microaggressions, they hear whining.

This does several things to the mixed race child, leaning on their white relatives for support as they navigate a racist world.

First, it creates failures of understanding. The non-white child learns that stories of microaggression will be treated as whining and be punished, and so she stops bringing home those stories. The white parent, grandparent, or other family member has no experience navigating the world as a person of color and so they do not know what the child is going through.

Second, the white family therefore cannot be a resource for the child. They cannot advocate for the child with teachers or administrators. They cannot call out little bits of racist bullshit. They cannot blow the whistle on treating Asian kids like model minorities or Black kids like troublemakers, because they have taught the child not to bring home the stories.

Third, not being a resource also means not helping the child combat the messages that they receive. I was talking, once, with a mixed race mentor and said something about feeling foolish for bringing my model minority issues up with a Black friend, especially since (unlike many Asian Americans), I have all the cultural capital of my white mother. My mentor pointed out that what I had not had was a family and a community seeing the racism that I experienced, and making sure that I knew I had value despite that racism. And it is true—what if you cannot tell the stories of racism to your white (or immigrant) parents, either because it is whining to do so, and we do not whine, or because it demonstrates a lack of gratitude for all that your immigrant parents gave up to give you a better life? Well, then they cannot combat the effects of that racism on your psyche.

And if you cannot talk about and be heard when you discuss racism that you experience in the world, if you are always being asked to consider the intent of the person in question, if you your nice white relatives cannot fathom that your nice white teacher/neighbor/minister/rabbi/doctor/soccer coach could be racist, you most certainly cannot call them out on the racism that you experience from them—even if that racism is simply composed of blind spots. For instance, the realization that they have worked so hard to give you women mentors, without (as far as you know) even noticing that you did not have Asian mentors.

Learning that it is "whining" to speak up about racism has a lasting effect as well. I currently have a white male supervisor who has never once gaslit me about racism. And I have never once managed to tell him about something without first panicking and assuming either that this will be the time he does not believe me, or that this will be the breaking point where, instead of being frustrated with the world we live in, he gets frustrated with me for whining. Or for making mountains out of molehills. Or for failing to care about intent. Or for deserving what was dished out to me.

Part of what can be complicated about sharing experiences of racism with white relatives comes, again, from their desire to show you that they understand, or even of their strong identification with you. For instance, after rarely talking about race, in the past few years, largely because of this book, I have tried to share stories with my mom about my life as a person of color. Of course, I am never just a person of color; I am always a South Asian–appearing woman without the cultural competency to play ball in the Indian world, educated in elite, primarily white institutions of higher education, single, without the financial or other support that comes with marriage, presumed (by non-academics) to have a financial standing more in line with other professionals. In academic circles, this is called "intersectionality," a term coined by legal scholar Kimberlé Crenshaw and defined by the Oxford English Dictionary as "the interconnected nature of social categorizations such as race, class, and gender as they apply to a given individual or group, regarded as creating overlapping and interdependent systems of discrimination or disadvantage." Sometime, when people imagine intersectionality, they think of it like an asterisk—that intersectionality is the point of intersection between, for instance, the problems of sexism and of racism. In this formulation, if you took all the problems that white women face, and all the problems that Black men face, you would understand the experience of Black women. But this is not quite right—intersectionality is all the overlapping pieces of identity, more than one could really isolate, but more importantly, it isn't really the sum total of oppressions, but rather the idea that these aspects of identity are all interconnected. What it is for me to be a woman is shaped by being straight, by being South Asian American, by having a white mother, by being of a certain economic and cultural class, by having a certain kind of education. But you cannot extract my womanness from my brownness—my being a woman is different for the fact that I am a brown woman, just as what it is for my mother to be a woman is shaped by her whiteness.

And this gets to the trouble: when I tell my mother about my experiences of racism, she often responds with stories about her life as a white woman. She tells me these stories so that she will be seen, but also to mirror to me that she hears me and understands me. I, however, am endlessly frustrated by this effort on her part, less because I am frustrated by my mother and more because I am frustrated in general by white women who think our experiences are analogous. Particularly when the women in question are white supervisors or mentors, who give advice based on their own life experience, unable to see that because of race, that advice might or might not work, and then what you have is a prescription that could cause problems for the person who tried to follow the advice, or problems if you do not. But when I point out differences, my mother wants to double down, or feels like, in my explanation that the experience of sexism and racism together is different from sexism alone, that I am playing a kind of misery poker that delegitimizes her experience. But more, she wants to demonstrate that she understands—she wants to reassure her child that I will never have to go through these experiences alone—and so she pulls from the experiences that she knows best. Even though I *am* alone in these experiences, or at least apart from her, and even though, as long as she insists on her examples as analogous experiences, her stories cannot really help me.

So, when I tell her that she will never understand what it is to live in a brown body, she asks me, defensively, then what is the point of art, of literature, of just listening to another person? And I try, when at my best, to explain that those things help with understanding, but always asymptotically—the understanding will never be perfect. Of course, this is always true in all types of human experiences—no matter what, we can never perfectly understand another's experience. We can never fully grasp what it is like to be in someone else's head. Sometimes, I try to use the example of sitting with a friend after her stillbirth. I explain to my mother that, after sitting with this friend for hours, over weeks, I understand better than I did before, and probably very well for someone who has never had or lost a child, what that experience of stillbirth is like. But I think we can all agree that it would be unreasonable for me to suggest that I completely understand, or that I ever could. Does my mother get this point? I'm not sure, although I know she's trying. I think that what is hardest for white loved ones to grasp is that the experience of a racialized body is something that they can sort of understand, but never internalize.

The idea that my mother does not and cannot understand completely hurts my mother. A friend of mine who is a mother says that this may be a place where, because I am not a mother, I may not be able to perfectly understand her—how much it hurts to know that not only can you not protect your children from the world, you cannot even quite share the world with them. My mother says, if she cannot understand something so fundamental to my experience, how can we be close? For me, however, when someone white insists that they understand, it makes me feel like closeness is impossible. It makes me feel farther apart—because not only do you not understand, you do not understand that you do not understand. You are not listening to me and hearing the shades of nuance in my description that are precisely the shades that I am trying to communicate.

My friends who are my age agree that we are close precisely because we name the not being able to understand. And that, for those of them who are white, they name that there is privilege in their not understanding. While my mother's lack of understanding is born of the same privilege, for her, I think that the not understanding is painful—it hurts her to know that there are pieces of her children's lives that she cannot see, and that because she cannot see them, she could not protect us from them. While I know no other mother-daughter relationship, at least not from the inside, and so I do not find our ability to attempt these conversations unusual, repeatedly, I hear from friends—particularly white friends, parenting non-white children, that they are surprised by the fact that we can broach these topics at all.

My mother has worked hard at hearing and understanding, and I have come to wonder whether my obsession with being heard and understood comes precisely from this gap between us. It is not just a gap; it is also loss embodied.

I think of one of my best friends, crying on the street as we walked home from dinner, talking about listening to the recording of Sandra Bland being pulled over. They said that, though they are queer, the fact that they are white and male-bodied meant that they could never imagine anyone, any cop, ever beginning to talk to them as the cop talked to Sandra Bland. Their tears did not feel like problematic white tears, because they were not demanding comfort, but rather tears of outrage and horror, at something that they had never even thought to imagine. And it is the never needing to imagine that is the part that can get in the way of understanding. It is hard to know what you do not understand, when you do not even know what you are failing to imagine.

And this is in part why, when I think about the ways that my white mother made sure that we knew about racism, I understand that it was almost always anti-Black racism that she referenced. There was a woman fired by American Airlines for having cornrows in the early 1990s. This made the news, and I can remember my mother banging pots and pans around in the kitchen, filled with fury about the racism. I remember the dinner table conversation about how it was racist to say that cornrows were not professional. But the reason that we were talking about this event was that it entailed a job loss. Similarly, no one was going to mistake the Rodney King beating for a microaggression. But the combination of only discussing newsworthy violence, police brutality, and loss of work with the sense that one should assume the best of others, not complain or tattle or whine, meant it was almost impossible for me to learn to navigate daily racism at that same table.

Five

APPROPRIATION

My grandfather came to the United States every time he got a new grandchild and sometimes in between. When he came, he usually stayed about six months, the length of a visitor's visa. Back in those days, my father was the only one of my grandfather's kids with a multi-bedroom house and a wife who would cook Indian vegetarian meals multiple times a day, so my grandfather spent most of that time with us. He was a man of routines. Every day, weather permitting, he would do yoga in our backyard. I can remember him in his kurta pajama, standing on his head on our red picnic table that my parents had built from a kit. He did not have a yoga mat—usually he would spread out a towel or blanket on the table, which put him at eyelevel for me, watching him through the back door. It was a storm door whose bottom third was metal, supporting the glass or screen top, which my mother would swap out with the seasons. I was little—I can remember the metal reaching shoulder height as I peered out at my strange and foreign grandfather.

This was probably a visit made in 1981, to celebrate my sister's first birthday. (My grandfather came to celebrate new grandchildren, but he was a lot of work and the sister-in-law in India did her best to keep him from showing up to visit and make work for her post-partum sisters-in-law in the US.) My mother had been reading *Alice in Wonderland* and *Through the Looking Glass* to me while she nursed the baby and she remembers coming upon me as I looked out at him and quietly reciting under my breath, "'You are old, Father William,' the young man said, 'and your hair has become very white. And yet you incessantly stand on your head. Do you think, at your age, it is right?'"

That was my introduction to yoga—I was three and a half years old, watching my grandfather doing headstands on the picnic table in a New England summer. There was no class, no teacher. My grandfather wore the same clothing that he stayed in all day, including for his long walks in the neighborhood, though he would often change into Levi's (which he considered the national dress of the United States) when he headed out to interact with the broader public. The yoga was the private, personal exercise and possibly spiritual routine of an elderly man who had ventured halfway around the world to visit his children in a world that he did not really understand. Now, as an adult, when I occasionally foray into the world of American yoga, I think of my grandfather on the back porch. I wonder what he would make of the dimly lit studios, the mandalas and Buddha statues, the expensive yoga mats and the Lululemon clothing—skin-tight and not something he would think his granddaughter should wear in public.

Every now and then, I try to take a yoga class. I do not take the class to feel close to my late grandfather, forever doing yoga in my memory, forever out there on our picnic table in a crisply ironed kurta pajama in the July sun. Quite frankly, I did not much know or like my grandfather. By the time I knew him, his English was rusty from retirement, so we did not have a language in common; and though he came to visit, he and my father did not get along. Late into the night, I would hear angry voices raised in a language I did not understand. So I am not trying to do yoga to get back to my roots or connect with my family.

I try for lots of reasons but principally because I move in the kind of liberal, educated circles in which yoga is something that people do. When I started working on this book, I lived in Mount Airy, a neighborhood in Philadelphia where I could walk to a food co-op whose health and pet annex sold yoga mats and Nag Champa incense. But more to the point, I am someone who has lived the kind of life—think political and social justice protests, folk festivals, pride parades (which are protest and festival), and small liberal arts colleges—that results in the ability to identify Nag Champa incense at just a whiff. I can also describe the box the incense was in—a sort of low-grade cardboard printed in unnatural indigo, somewhere on the line between purple and blue. Now I work in Boulder, where Nag Champa incense abounds. But in my day, I have also lived in Cambridge (Massachusetts), Brooklyn, and a hippie neighborhood in Atlanta, where I belonged to a synagogue in which someone once organized an event where we got up before sunrise to mark a cool solar event with yoga and improvised Jewish ritual at the highest point in Grant Park before all of us headed out for breakfast. I often cannot afford, but swear by, acupuncture, at least for certain maladies. (I did not believe in it until a friend in acupuncture school needed to practice on someone and, figuring, what the hell, I let her practice on me—and she repeatedly relieved my migraines and headed colds off at the pass.) I once chose a gym because it had a pool that had dimmed lights and played, if not literally Enya, then

Enya-esque music. (If you timed it right, you could swim end-less laps without having to share the lane, which I also liked. But I really loved the Enya.)

And besides, I have chronic back pain and notable anxiety. Of course I have tried yoga. I work in Boulder. My first month in town, someone recommended a different yoga studio every day. But for all my hippie-dippie tendencies, something always goes wrong when I set foot in a yoga studio. And I have tried lots of yoga studios. I have tried power yoga with music blar-ing in New York City; I have tried yoga in darkened rooms in Reading, Pennsylvania, where the mats have been replaced with wool blankets that might harbor germs and certainly har-bor the faint aroma of Nag Champa incense; and I have tried yoga at the gym with the Enya pool, in a room that resembled a ballet studio, where, at night, headlights lit the darkened room and you could smell pizza from the restaurant next door. I have popped into Bikram yoga in Decatur, Georgia, and once, while staying with a college friend in Berkeley, I followed him to a yoga class filled with people who had such a high level of skill that, before they were done warming up, I had gone prone, in corpse pose, having cried "uncle" on the entire experience. (When I did not get up after a few minutes, I realized that someone was looking at me, and I opened my eyes to the wor-ried gaze of my friend Ben.) What I am saying here is that I am not very good at yoga, quite terrible, really, but I have tried it—many times. And in many settings.

I never go back for a second, or fifth, class. With the ex-ception of the class in Berkeley, where I was not offended but simply out of my depth (and just passing through), my failure or refusal to return is because, at some point in the process, something goes awry.

So, to be filed under things that ruin yoga for me: to begin with, chanting. In Sanskrit, in a class that had no discussion of chanting, I remember a class that ended with the teacher and all the students chanting "om." The teacher, and the more advanced students, or just the repeat customers, may have, at some point, had a more advanced class on chanting, but I had just walked in off the street. Certainly, I had identified the gayatri mantra on the sound system during the class. When that happens, I always think, people in this room who are not Catholic, how would you feel if, all of a sudden, in the middle of an aerobics class, or a series of gentle stretches, someone asked you to recite the Hail Mary? People in this room who *are* Catholic, how would you feel if this room, filled with people who are not Catholic, also did so? What would you think if you also knew that they secretly (or not so secretly) looked down on Catholics, implicitly thought of them as less American? Would doing it in Latin make it okay? I know, from every time I have ever been to an airport in a post 9–11 world, that generally speaking, white people, whatever they think theoretically about racial profiling by TSA, do not object when I am pulled aside for extra screening. And those are the thoughts that pop into my mind at such moments in yoga, along with wondering what my grandmother, whom I never met, but who was reputed to be very devout and a strict vegetarian, would think of all of these people who chant "om" and also eat beef.

There is, of course, quite a bit of writing out there on appropriation—lots of hot takes about how it is wrong, and bad. And sometimes, "appropriation is bad" is exactly the case: I am happy to get in line with the "my culture is not your costume" concept, particularly when the costume is rooted in stereotype and sold cheaply on Amazon. But I also like cultural exchange. I like learning about other cultures, experiencing them, and being shaped and changed by them. I like cooking Jamaican peas and rice with thyme and coconut milk, a recipe I received from Dianne, the woman who also taught me to teach and to navigate the academic world as a woman of color. I do not like to meditate, but I am a better person when I do so, and I am grateful to the monks and nuns who taught me to do so in a Taiwanese monastery. And honestly, I dislike meditating enough that I probably would not have pushed through and developed the skill if I had not been stuck, far from public transportation, in a place where I could not speak the language. And while I was there, eating my meals in total silence, with slippery metal chopsticks, I was grateful for the high school friends who had patiently taught me to use chopsticks.

Where then, is the line between cultural exchange or influence and cultural appropriation? How does it work? Why is it that I think cultural exchange is good, want to do yoga, and cannot stand to be with yoga people? How is all of this true? Where are the lines? And how do we think about where the lines should be, for us, or for those times when we are deciding with whom to be mildly miffed, annoyed, or seriously angry?

I also have a beef with white ladies wearing Indian clothing.

I can point to the day that I developed my white-ladies-in-saris allergy. After all, my mother is white, so I grew up seeing a white woman in a sari fairly regularly—any time we went to a community or family function. Functions are what Indians call parties above a certain size. A function is anything for which one might drive a distance or dress up, and a kind of gathering that characterizes so much of Indian American life. But my particular allergy to white women in saris came upon me suddenly, like breaking out in hives after a lifetime of eating strawberries with no prior histamine reaction. The problem first showed up at a wedding in Cambridge the summer of 2001. And it came on while I, myself, was wearing a sari wrapped by a white woman.

The bride and groom were married in the New England church where they were both deeply engaged in the community. Because of their community involvement and the pride that they knew the congregation felt in these two young adults who had found each other at church, the couple decided to invite the entire congregation to their wedding ceremony and a lemonade-and-finger-foods reception afterward. Later that night, they held a more formal wedding supper with dinner and dancing for out-of-town guests. But people who were at the daytime wedding and tea were wearing the kind of clothing that people normally wear to church.

A number of the young women from the congregation's young adult group asked the bride if she would mind if they wore saris to the wedding. Many of them, as it turned out, had traveled to India (not together, as far as I know), and, enticed by the beautiful silk saris that they saw, had brought some home. Of course, they never had a chance to wear them, as they did not particularly have Indian friends—or, at least, were not braided into the Indian community such that they went to events where Indian clothing is the norm. As a result, they said, they were having a sari party later that afternoon. They really wanted to attend the wedding but were afraid that they would not have time to go home and get ready for their sari party.

The bride mentioned these saris to me when I asked if she would mind if I wore a sari to the wedding. I was wearing a sari partly for the same reason that the other women were: I have some and I rarely have a chance to wear them. But mostly I was wearing a sari because I was twenty-three and I could not afford, on my AmeriCorps salary, a dress for my friend's wedding. I did, however, have access to my mother's saris. Saris are one-size-fits-all, and my mother knows how to sew sari blouses and could therefore alter or make one for me. I, however, am not good at wrapping saris. I took my sari, carefully pressed by a small-town Connecticut drycleaner who has been doing my mom's saris for years to the church before the wedding. The matron of honor, who, like my mom, was a white woman married to an Indian man, wrapped my sari for me, with knife-edge pleats at my waist and over my chest, with carefully hidden pins holding them in place.

When I arrived at the church for the wedding, I noticed the clutch of women bound for the sari party later. They wore their saris draped like togas at a frat party. While they had bought the lovely yards of silk, the underpinnings had not interested them. Black leotards and nylon bathing suits peeked out from under their saris. I can't be sure what held up the bottom part of their saris, but my guess is that the women had tied ropes or shoelaces around their waists and tucked the fabric into them. Either way, the fabric was rumpled and the pleats bunched, wadded into some sort of waistband. They had not pinned their *palloos*, the piece of the sari to hang down the back, drape the head, or lie pleated over the chest. These women all had wrapped their saris with the palloo hanging down the back and kept having to push them up over their shoulders. In short, they wore their saris as costumes, with no real respect for the idea that there is an etiquette to saris, just as there is to any other mode of dress. As the matron of honor's husband said to me while we gathered birdseed to toss at the bride and groom, it was an insult to the fabric. It was rude, it was disrespectful, it was kind of like ethnic Halloween costumes—only somehow it struck me as worse because the women weren't even acting like they were in costume.

At the buffet line, one of the women bent over to dish up some food, and her sari slid off her shoulder. She pushed it up, glanced over at me, and said, "I see you remembered your pin." On some level, I felt like she was accusing me of cheating—like having training wheels on a bike, or rubber bands on chopsticks, or some other mode of childishness. But in reality, while many people can and do manage saris without pins, to me going pin-less is like leaving the house without your bra on—you might be able to get away with it; you might even look good; but for better or for worse, and politics aside, a lot of people basically will not think your attire is acceptable. And while one might be able to pass without a pin, substituting a leotard because of the lack of a proper sari blouse is much more akin to leaving the house without a shirt than without an undergarment. It is like putting on a suit over a men's white undershirt—the kind that you can also use to substitute for cheese cloth.

So, clearly, there is a line here. The issue is not so much white ladies in saris as it is the respect or disrespect that those ladies showed toward the clothing. The issue is also the respect that these women were or were not showing to the bride by showing up in these outfits. (My mom's next-door neighbor once threw a party where you were supposed to wear your ugliest brides-maid's dress. It was an excellent party idea, but I find myself wondering: if this group of guests had been heading off to an "ugly bridesmaid's dress party," would they have asked a bride if they could wear out-of-date bridesmaid's dresses? Would they have asked if the dresses no longer fit, or were missing crinolines, and so were not zipped up all the way or hung fun-nily? I think that we all know the answer to that question.)

It is not, in fact, that I always object to a white lady in a sari. I firmly believe that my mother earned every single one of her saris in her forty years as my father's wife, or more importantly, the half of those years that were also spent as my grandfather's daughter-in-law, which provided a more complete immersion in some of the more unfortunate aspects of Indian culture. I also have no problem with the white ethnographer of religion in my graduate program who often wore Indian clothing to work. Even before I knew her personal story, my professor and her approach did not particularly bother me—probably because, long before I knew that she had grown up in India, I saw that she could manage both a sari and a dupata with a grace that I couldn't begin to imitate. Both my mother and Joyce, my professor, can wrap a sari with knife-edge pleats that fall down the front and over their shoulders. They both know where to place a discreet pin. My mother once wrapped me into a sari so well that I managed to swing dance at a family wedding without getting particularly ruffled.

When I asked Joyce her thoughts, she said that she thinks that proficiency is key—wearing a sari is a specific skill, and when she does so, people can tell that she has invested in the process. She also pointed to understanding timing and context: what clothing do you wear—and when do you wear it? At one point, when Joyce was living in India, she visited with a friend who worked at the US Embassy. As she explained it, the State Department had forbidden its employees to wear traditional Indian clothing while on official State Department work, including receptions and parties. Joyce said that, at first, this policy offended her, partly on behalf of her friend, who would have worn Indian clothing well. But then she learned the reason behind the policy: apparently, the problem was that people kept getting it wrong and wearing clothing inappropriate to the setting. I am guessing that many of these people were women, because in India, as in the United States, the social codes and assumptions embedded in women's clothing are more formal and nuanced than they are for men. After all, I have at least twenty black dresses, ranging from what I wear to the beach to what I wore to my best friend's wedding. I have dresses to wear to drinks with friends and dresses to wear for teaching, both of which differ from the dresses that you would wear to a boardroom meeting or to the farmer's market—and few of which could be worn to church, a wedding, a Christmas party, or a disco. Clothing is hard.

Joyce did not explain whether these women were getting it wrong because, like the women who went to the wedding, they were attracted to the beautiful fabrics and did not care about context, or whether they simply found the nuances too hard to grasp. It could be the latter. I find that, as a northeasterner, I sometimes wear the wrong clothes when I travel to other parts of the United States—I wear the wrong black dress, for instance, because I do not realize that church in Georgia is a shade more bridal shower and a bit less office attire, or because I did not realize that the dinner party was a barbecue. How much harder it is when the items of clothing—and the subtle implications of color, fabric, and trimming—do not come from our own culture.

Part of why I do not mind white ladies wearing Indian clothing, then, or why at least I do not mind when these women are my mom and my professor, is that both of them *know* Indian clothing. They can match the outfit to the context and setting. Joyce never came to work dressed for a party—she knows that Indian clothing, like American clothing, has a context and a dress code, and she dressed for work in what my aunts (blood and close family friends) wear to work in schools and law firms and at the United Nations. My mother never really wears workday Indian clothing, but she understands that a cookout at my aunt's house is not a wedding. She has saris for garden parties and saris for housewarmings and dinner parties and weddings.

Knowledge, then, is part of what seems central to the discussion of appropriation. What my mother and Joyce both have, and the ladies at the wedding did not have (or were not exhibiting, if they did have it), is knowledge of how a culture works, what should happen and what should not. Implicit in that is respect—respect for a culture and how it functions.

It is more than knowledge, though. Here is the other thing about my white mother's experience, marrying my thirty-three-year-old Indian immigrant father when she was only twenty-two years old. As far as I can tell, she was expected to learn to be the perfect Indian daughter-in-law. If being my father's wife was anything like being his daughter, sometimes she was supposed to be the perfect American wife and other times, the perfect Indian wife. She learned how to cook, and how to wrap a sari. Once, my dad brought home some guys from the Pakistani Merchant Marine, whom he had found lost in Bridgeport, Connecticut. They needed dinner, it was late at night, and they spoke Urdu and not English. My father brought them home. My mom cooked them a full Indian dinner, with multiple dishes and homemade, individually rolled-out chapatis. When my mom tells this story, it is cute: I wanted one of the men to read me a book, and he was embarrassed because he could not read English. The next day, she was invited to see their ship, and they put on dress uniforms and she got to walk through a tunnel made of swords. It is a great story and I have always loved it. But as an adult, I find myself thinking: out of loyalty basically to the Urdu language, my dad brought home a bunch of male total strangers from the merchant marine of his country of origin's most bitter enemy. He did this late at night. And he expected his twenty-nine-year-old pregnant wife to get up, out of bed, and cook an elaborate meal for these strange men, with whom she lacked a language. And the entire process had me awake past my bedtime, which also means that at some point, she probably found herself home alone, pregnant, with a fussier-than-otherwise toddler.

And she did all of it at the risk of severe criticism if she failed. When my mom married Daddy, my grandfather wanted to change her name from Linda to Lakshmi, which, according to the customs of my father's community, he had every right to do. (In fact, one of my father's cousins married a man whose sister had the same name that she did, and so her new in-laws did change her name. Her husband had the sense to get himself and his new bride transferred to a different city, so that they could escape the joint family, and my sense is that they had a very happy marriage and he called her by her birth name. I have no idea if his family ever did.) My dad's youngest sister headed off the name change, but that moment represents the sort of assimilation that my father's family attempted to ask of my mother.

In many ways, my father did not ask that level of assimilation from her (though the merchant marine story gives you a sense of how, in some ways he did), and Daddy was eager to be an American, but it is also true that he was, in many ways, haunted. My father was the second, less favored son, the bad seed longing to be the prodigal, and so he was forever searching for approval from his family of origin. When you combine that with his alcoholism and its attendant boundary problems, he almost always put the needs and, perhaps more problematically, the desires of his father and siblings, and extended kin, ahead of the needs of my mother and her children. Because it is true that Indian culture has a strong emphasis on obligation to extended family, in comparison to the US's emphasis on nuclear family, I, and I suspect my mother, could never quite tell what were my father and his family's pathology and lack of boundaries, and what was cultural difference. I know, however, that my father often presented his approach as rooted in cultural difference, and he expected my mother to be the one who should accommodate that difference. I am almost positive that, when he and his family framed things that way, they undercut her ability to negotiate boundaries that felt right to her. And her inability to negotiate those boundaries had big stakes, in terms of how she (and we) spent our time. Ultimately, they even undercut her financial security. My mother has both learned a huge amount about Indian culture and has had Indian culture used against her, when family dysfunction has been presented as cultural difference.

But what rights do these personal experiences give? My mother has talked about writing about her experience with my father's family, either in memoir or in fiction, using the name that my grandfather tried to give her. She has talked about taking on this name in part for the anonymity—the ability to have a nom de plume and not be caught out by the relatives— but also because an Indian name might give her credibility in writing on Indian topics. Such a move is no longer possible, in an age of book tours and the internet, but when she floated this idea, I explained that it was not possible, or appropriate, for a white woman to assume an Indian name, in the guise of gaining authority. When I tried to explain this, and said, "you can't do that! It is too much like colonialism," she reminded me that my grandfather had tried to force this name on her. "I felt like Papaji was colonizing me," she responded.

And here is the thing: I imagine that she did. And, in the power dynamics of her marriage, my white mother, in her native country, was also largely at the mercy of her husband and their respective patriarchal cultures. By virtue of his authority, as husband and provider (he out-earned her until he retired), by virtue of his being ten years older and having a more domineering personality, he had most of the power in their marriage. She learned his culture, and lived with some of its finer points, but also its flaws and failings. What would she need to do to be seen as an authority on it? Without him next to her now, how could she still inhabit the pieces that she wants to retain?

My mother understands the dangers of being, essentially, Rachel Dolezal, and, quite frankly, never really meant to pass herself off as anything other than who and what she is. Using the name that my grandfather tried to use to erase her was a way of taking back that bit of erasure, but also a way of saying, "I learned, I adapted, I know what I am talking about." The idea that she would pass as Indian was a joke, and not one that I thought was particularly funny—I was angry at my white mother for thinking she could inhabit my positionality when she wanted to and exit it when she did not, and nervous that she did not understand the political stakes or the pain in her joke. And, as soon as she understood, she backed off. But also, what do we do with the fact that our political moment does not allow space for her to joke about the pain that she experienced, precisely as she fit into another culture.

To my grandfather, my mother would have shown Indian culture more respect if she had taken the name that he tried to give her. To me, she would be showing Indian American culture less respect if she tried to claim that name now.

But, even within the context of multifaceted American culture, respect is complicated. What feels respectful on the part of the person taking on a practice might not feel respectful to the person whose culture is being taken on. In this sense, then, appropriation is, on some level, always in the eye of the beholder. I am thinking about the 2015 blowup about whether it was appropriation for Oberlin College to serve bad Asian (or other ethnic) food in the cafeteria. My opinion? It wasn't appropriation. It was an attempt to be inclusive—either that, or it was the product of an American culture in which many Oberlin students come from cities and are used to ethnic food, and here they are in small-town Ohio, and they don't like what they're eating. Was the food terrible? Probably. I mean, why wouldn't it have been? It was a dining hall. Look me in the eye and tell me that the pasta, fried chicken, and vegan stuffed peppers were not also wretched. If dining hall food is like home cooking, there is something wrong with your home. The steam trays alone do in the most basic attempt at a decent meal.

Thinking about appropriation also makes me remember my friend Shreena's favorite story about me from college—she is part of my chosen family now, but we barely knew each other back then. Shreena is a friend who is always there to help me see when my experiences are tinged with racism, is generally far more woke than I am, and is also a scholar of Hinduism in America who writes about yoga, culture appropriation, and white supremacy. She loves to tell the story of a Divali meal at the Swarthmore College dining hall. Someone from the Indian students' group (I think the Indian students' group hosted because in the story, Shreena says "we," but I was not part of the "we," so that sounds like the Indian students' group to me) had finagled money from the college to decorate the dining hall and to have an "Indian meal" cooked by the dining hall staff. (To my dying day, I will remember their Indian-inspired chickpeas—those were not a special treat—that showed up on the vegetarian food line at least one week each month. But on one of the non-vegetarian lines there was, apparently, a beef curry.) In Shreena's memory, and I have no reason to think she is exaggerating, I walked up to her as she was eating her beef curry, full of indignation that the dining hall was serving beef on this important Hindu holiday. Whenever Shreena tells this story, she mimes that she was actually eating the beef as I said this, and says that she declared, "No. No I cannot believe that. It is really horrible that they would do that." I, meanwhile, either did not notice her beef or did not call her on this—I remember the decorations, but nothing about the food or the exchange. So, I cannot say whether I did not notice, or did notice after I spoke and pretended not to see.

But here is the thing: to the two of us, this moment in the dining hall was a moment, not of cultural appropriation, but of cultural acceptance. Divali was being celebrated—just like we had pumpkin cookies at Halloween and Christmas cookies at Christmas, and extra chocolate at Valentine's Day. And if they made what some might think of as a mistake—if serving beef on a Hindu holiday was like the year we realized that the matzo that they had stacked up for Passover was not actually Kosher for Passover, well, I might have been the only person who minded. Shreena, whose affiliation with Hinduism is much stronger than mine, eats beef all the time and did not mind at all. Maybe they were not making a mistake—maybe they were fulfilling a full range of Hindu dietary practices, from those who got beef from one food line to those who got "pure veg" from another. Regardless, the Indian food was terrible—but it was not more terrible than the pasta or the tacos, and it made us feel like our holidays were honored by the community.

So, food essentially does not bother me. Granted, I would be a terrible hypocrite if I wanted to ding people for eating ethnic food when I would happily eat yemisir wot at least once a week (and leftovers for lunch the next day) for the rest of my life. But also, Shreena and I do come from households with different habits around meat. Before I betrayed my father by becoming a vegetarian, he had taught me to like filet mignon, but in my family, beef was to be kept separate from Hindu holidays and events. That was not where it belonged. In Shreena's family, it was not kept separate. And so, in this case, we disagreed about whether there was a problem. But even with my complaints, I did not think the meal was appropriation.

When I think about why I am not, in the end, bothered by the example of dining hall food, or ethnic restaurants, I find myself thinking of what Amanda Lucia has to say about these broader themes, when, in her book *White Utopias*, she writes, "Historically, cultural encounter, whether by trade or warfare, often involves the exchange of cultural forms; many of these moments of cultural exchange occur outside of the context of whiteness. But the notion of cultural appropriation focuses attention on individual white actors and their representative claims of non-white cultural and religious forms. Cultural appropriation is an individualized expression of an overarching institutionalized system that expresses white access and ownership." Part of what I like about Lucia's comments is that they help me to tease out what is going on when I think that what I am seeing is cultural exchange, and what is going on when I think I see appropriation.

Central here is the idea of power—and the understanding that cultural exchange happens within the broader power dynamic. Personally, I like cultural exchange—to stick, for a moment with the example of food: I like ethnic restaurants (though I worry about labor practices), but there is a difference between going to the local (pick your ethnicity) mom-and-pop restaurant or buying a cookbook written by a member of a culture (say, the Madhur Jaffery *Invitation to Indian Cooking* that my mom used as the basis for recipes painstakingly adapted to my father's specifications of his dead mother's dishes) and the kerfuffle that occurred over Alison Roman.

The Alison Roman scandal revolved around appropriation. In the spring of 2020, as the United States (and much of the world) embraced home cooking in the face of the global pandemic, Alison Roman, food writer for the *New York Times* and *Bon Appétit*, put her foot in it about race. She disparaged two Asian or Asian American celebrities for creating product lines, calling them sellouts in the same interview in which she touted her own product line. (She also did not criticize any number of white celebrities with lifestyle brands.) Judgment followed, swift and harsh. But as Roxana Hadadi, cultural critic and senior editor at *Pajiba* pointed out, in her article "Alison Roman, the Colonization of Spices, and the Exhausting Prevalence of Ethnic Erasure in Popular Food Culture," that moment of overt racism, bad as it was, was not actually the biggest problem with Roman. The biggest problem with Roman, Hadadi argued, is that she pulls recipes from other cultures and then denies that she has done so—as in the case of Roman's "The Stew." The Stew (capital *T*, capital *S*) is, basically, a cross between a South Asian chana masala—a dish my mom made all the time when I was growing up and, to this day, my favorite thing to get her to make—and a West Indian chickpea curry. The problem, as Hadadi points out, is not that Roman is a white woman making a South Asian/West Indian dish. The problem is not that she potentially stripped the recipe down, either to make the flavors blander for the US palate or easier and quicker to make after work. The problem is that she denied that her recipe had a history. She did not identify its roots, and then when people called her on it, she denied that her stew was a curry. Hadadi quotes her as saying, "Y'all, this is not a curry. . . . I've never made a curry; I don't come from a culture that knows about curry. I come from no culture. I have no culture. I'm like, vaguely European." This is not how Hadadi puts it, but basically, lady, that means that you come from a culture that does not know about turmeric, ginger, or coconut, and yet they are all right there in your recipe. More to the point, Europeans do know about curry, largely through a history of colonialism. But also, lady, cite your sources.

One of Hadadi's best phrases shows up when she writes, "Roman's refusal to acknowledge the groups and people that she is pulling from allows her to present herself as the sole authority on these kinds of foods." When Roman describes herself as without culture, this reference is "not self-deprecating, not really. It's a way to absorb other people's identities and present them as her own expertise, and her expertise only. And if I may be extremely cynical, it allows Roman to play to a certain kind of reader. Someone who doesn't want to make Indian food because, ew, it's smelly, or Chinese food because, ew, they eat bats, or Iranian food because, ew, they're terrorists. Roman gets to be the next great white hope."

Hadadi's critique is fair. Roman is, essentially, stripping food of its culture in order to make it more sellable to people who can then enhance their lives with other people's cuisine without having to encounter the people, or stretch themselves and rethink their existing prejudices. Yet Roman's comment about not having culture herself is also her justification for the very appropriation she denies. When she presents herself as culturally impoverished, she is giving herself license to venture out and acquire other people's culture. Yet—and this is important for white Americans to grasp—she *does* have a culture: it is merely invisible to her, in the same way that (we assume) fish do not notice water or we do not notice air. Everyone has a culture. Being a white American who is "vaguely European" does not mean that you lack a culture. You may not know your European heritage, but Americans have culture.

Culture is why Northerners think that Southern friendliness is fake and Southerners think that Northern reserve is rude. It is why most of us know, from watching and listening to them, that Fran Lebowitz is from New York and Garrison Keillor is from Minnesota. It is country music, jazz, and the American folk tradition. It is Minnesota hot dish, Cincinnati chili on spaghetti, and debates over whether there should be sugar in cornbread. It is maple syrup on pancakes. There are aspects of this culture that you might not want to think about or claim (minstrel shows or rape culture or crushing credit card debt, for example), but they too are part of your culture.

Hadadi talks about how chefs of color do not (sometimes) care if the white cook in question has really learned the history or culture of a food—they point out that when their immigrant or enslaved parents undertook such learning themselves upon arrival in the United States, they did so out of necessity; no one thought it was a virtue. Here, I am not so sure. I do not think Julia Child was acceptable exclusively because she was white and the French are (often) white. I think Child was—and still is—acceptable because she really learned and acknowledged French recipes and technique. She went to the Cordon Bleu. She put the French right there in her title, *Mastering the Art of French Cooking*. I also get the point—it is annoying when the cultural ambassador who is earning the money and getting to be the face of a recipe is white and not a person of color. There is a reason why I was so excited when Francis Lam took over NPR's the *Splendid Table*, or why I am comfortable at all buying a copy of *Sioux Chef*, for the knowledge that Sean Sherman is Lakota. (I also like his organizational mission.)

But leaving aside someone like Sherman, whose work presents his own food culture and who has an entire nonprofit dedicated to serving the Indigenous community, what about people cooking across culinary traditions? Samin Nosrat's television version of *Salt, Fat, Acid, Heat*, where she highlights cooks and voices from specific cultures, offers a counterpoint to Roman. One can imagine a charge of exoticism—Nosrat tends toward the artisanal, which implies an old-school and potentially unchanging foreign past, but not one of appropriation. (And even then, Nosrat is not actually gesturing to an unchanging alien world. An elderly cook explains that her children and grandchildren do not do it this way; a soy sauce manufacturer explains that what makes his product unique is that he does it the old way, and so forth.) Nosrat is not acceptable, not so much because, as an Iranian American, she is not (necessarily) white—in interviews she talks about how, legally, she is white—but because, functionally, she has often not been read as white. Rather when she presents Mexican, Japanese, or Italian food, she deeply roots them in Mexico, Japan, or Italy. She presents herself not as the inventor of the food she introduces, or even as its discoverer, but rather as a deeply knowledgeable student of cuisine who has come to learn from culinary, and therefore cultural, experts. And having done that, she buys herself credibility when she creates fusion food, for instance, what she refers to on her podcast *Home Cooking* as Japanese Fusion Samin Style.

Cultural theorist Amanda Lucia is helpful here too, in thinking about what happens when an encounter is shaped by power imbalance, when only those with power get to speak (or get to speak the loudest), and when they speak without regard to other points of view. "Utopian versions of religious exoticism," she writes, "are defined by a particular notion of the other. In its most idyllic form, the other is romanticized as an untouched essence—timeless, pure, and uncorrupted by modernity . . . Furthermore, religious exoticism's perseverating focus on the purity, timelessness, and authenticity of the other necessarily dissociates it from the actual communities that practice the religious forms that it adopts." To make something exotic is to suggest, in part, that it is static and premodern. When a culture or a person is exoticized, there is neither room for complex emotional realities or for changing and dynamic culture. That is why one could argue that the Netflix special *Salt, Fat, Acid, Heat* is exoticizing. When Nosrat interviews the people who make soy sauce the way it has been made for centuries, rather than taking us to a soy sauce plant, she is, perhaps, offering a picture of a timeless and exotic Japan. On the other hand, she is careful to point out that this is not, in fact, how most soy sauce is actually made. She is, in essence, taking us to see something in its boutique form, or teaching us culinary history through a boutique revival. While Nosrat's relationship to exoticism might be complex, Roman's is not.

At first glance, it might seem that Lucia and Hadadi are making two very different points—Hadadi is criticizing Roman for making curry palatable to people who think ethnic food is weird, while Lucia is talking about people who turn to "ethnic" religion precisely *because* it is "weird," that is, exotic. Put another way, Roman receives criticism for deliberately playing down the exotic, while Lucia's observed subjects are deliberately playing it up—yet both are erasing the real people and expertise involved in their cultures and communities.

This erasure is not, in the end, neutral. In some ways, that seems like a totally obvious thing to say—that erasure is not neutral—but let us think a bit about what precisely that means. First, what Roman is doing actually enables people to benefit from the wonderful diversity of the world without having to be decent about it—you can have the delicious food without having to confront your own prejudices, take cultural offerings without having to have any responsibility to be in good relationship with the people in question. Second, if you are Roman, you are essentially making money off cultures without citing your sources.

What are the implications of those erasures? One implication is what Lucia writes about—the possibility of reducing a person or a community to an exotic abstraction. Several years ago, I read, and was infuriated by, *The Saffron Cross*, a memoir by J. Dana Trent, a white woman "ordained in the Southern Baptist tradition," about her interfaith marriage to a man she describes as a "Western-born former Hindu monk." Trent constantly frames her own Christianity as a "Western, Protestant materialistic perspective" in contrast to Hinduism, "a daily framework of humble service to God." Trent presents her husband's Hinduism as a countercultural (at least counter to Western culture) religion of a simple living, shaped by monasticism (even if her husband and some of his friends are no longer monks) and separated from familial and social obligations. Because her husband's Hinduism is that of a white convert, it is, in fact, more free from familial obligations—as his family does not celebrate Divali, his experience of the holiday is what he wants it to be, and not what his family expects. Trent presents (and suggests that her husband presented to her) this version of Hinduism as the religion, in its essence. In her telling, Hinduism serves as an anti-materialist rebuke to a Christianity that has lost its way in American strip malls. Trent's take on Hinduism is one that may map onto her husband's experience as a white convert, but it does not take into account the reality that the people on the television show *Indian Matchmaker* are often Hindu, as are the Patels in the documentary *Meet the Patels*. In both, people are deeply conscious of many things of which Trent would disapprove: economic class, religious caste, skin color (much is made, here, of the wheatish completion). These, however, are central pieces on which many traditional Hindu marriages are made. Would Trent argue that these people are not Hindu, or that they are bad Hindus? The wealthy and extravagant *Monsoon Wedding* people are Hindu, as are my cousins, whose automotive choices cost more than any house I can see myself buying in any realistic version of my future.

But what does it mean, really mean, to fail to account for people? As Lucia's work demonstrates, the countercultural forms of Hinduism and Buddhism in the United States end up being predominantly white spaces, separate from the Hinduism of immigrant communities. Liberal people who espouse values like diversity end up creating communities that are just as white as their right-wing counterparts, partly because they have created versions of "Eastern" religions in which "Eastern" people cannot see themselves, and partly because Asian people, with their takes on Hinduism and Buddhism that include stories of crass materialism, homophobia, meddlesome aunts, conservative asshole uncles, misogyny, racism, and classism, disrupt the utopic versions of "Eastern" religions that the white liberals are using to counter their own struggles against much the same. We all have meddlesome aunts; conservative asshole uncles; third cousins who comment on our weight, or our marital or reproductive status; Hinduism and Buddhism, like Christianity and Judaism, contain misogyny, racism, and classism. But, in the end, counterculture takes on Hinduism and Buddhism exist in part to be spaces where white people can imagine themselves to be purified of all of those things. And so, if your brown Hinduism comes complete with homophobic grandmothers or if you experience and call out racism in the utopic space that the white devotees have created, it is you that has to go or to be silenced.

But these things matter, even for those of us who do not actually want to go to Burning Man or Shaktifest. (To be clear, I maybe sort of *do* want to go to Burning Man or Shaktifest. Or maybe I don't. I like privacy, and I do not really like lots of sand in my sleeping bag. But I also like hippie folk festivals and camping. At the same time, I can tell that I would not like *these* hippie folk festivals. It is partly that they sound self-indulgent, but mostly they sound like too much exoticization and not enough Pete Seeger, of blessed memory.) In Trent's case in *The Saffron Cross*, her failure to account for actual people left her free to make observations like the following: "Even during India's coldest months of December and January, hardly anyone wears a coat. Poverty is one reason for this bizarre practice; being a colorful, joyful people is the other. In India, it's much more acceptable to wear mismatching layers of saris and chaddars that boast swirls of rainbow colors than a boring winter coat. This is India's paradox—vibrancy amidst heartache." Her argument here is that, in India, people would rather be cold than wear a coat. This idea that Indians are joyful, as expressed in their bright clothing, and that white Americans are not, as expressed in our blacks and grays, is a strange assertion. Joy and sorrow exist everywhere, and to call a people "colorful" and "joyous" to the point of failure to protect against cold is to suggest that they are childlike.

The fixation on bright colors as a contrast to the blacks and navys and grays of an imagined stream of Westerners in metaphorical bowler hats is odd. My first year as a professor, I met a visiting scholar in the English department. She was there on a fellowship year, teaching a class or two and leading enrichment activities for faculty. Together, we read a collection of novels by Indian and Indian American writers, and, in at least one case, a collection of short stories, Jhumpa Lahiri's Pulitzer Prize–winning debut collection *The Interpreter of Maladies*. One of the short stories, "Mrs. Sen's," tells the story of a woman whose marriage has brought her from India to New England. Mrs. Sen's loneliness and out-of-placeness are represented by her saris. As we started to discuss, one of the other English professors exclaimed, "It must be so hard for people from India to come here and leave all of those beautiful colors for our black and gray and navy blue." In retrospect, it is hard for me to pin down what fell apart for me in that moment, but I do remember how deeply annoyed I was. There was something about the statement, as if, in India, no women had ever felt glamorous in black or as if, in the US, no woman had ever worn a red sequined dress. I caught my colleague Jennifer's glance, and we rolled our eyes. While Jennifer was wearing a black top, under the table, her skirt was a range of peacock greens and blues. Tossed over a chair in the corner was my hot-pink coat, bought at a very exotic location—an Ann Taylor Loft in Atlanta. It was the attitude of my colleague that galled me—as if Indian women, once in the United States, could not figure out where they could buy bright colors. Just like my colleague who seems to think we force black and navy coats on people, Trent seems unable to see that poverty, not moral purity or a dedication to the picturesque, prevents people from buying an expensive winter coat that they will only need for two weeks of the year.

That said, appearance *does* matter, and it does connect to culture, and social location. My friend Chrissy Lau is an activist and historian who spent the COVID-19 pandemic sewing with the Auntie Sewing Squad, a group founded by Asian American performance artist and comedian Kristina Wong to provide masks to people who needed them, focusing on those in vulnerable communities. They sewed for people on reservations, for migrant farmworkers, and for the incarcerated. In doing so, "Auntie" Chrissy says that they have learned what it means to listen to the people for whom they are sewing. She wrote to me in a text, "for residents of Native American reservations, they asked us to stay away from specific colors or patterns (prints with specific animals) because it aligned with their spiritual beliefs and traditions. They also asked us to stay away from anything related to indigenous cultural appropriation." Meanwhile, incarcerated women often appreciated traditionally feminine colors and prints—pinks and florals were popular, lace and sparkles appreciated. The point here is not that members of a community might have shared tastes, shaped by cultural conventions or social locations. It is simply that we might need to listen to these community members pretty closely to know what those tastes are.

In the case of South Asians, and I assume, many, many other people, part of what this not-listening means is assuming that you understand "their" culture (and also probably assuming that the culture is singular, which is another problem altogether). It means assuming that you do not have to do the kind of attentive listening that Auntie Chrissy describes. In 2015, when an elementary school in Georgia introduced a yoga class to de-stress students (which we should be worrying about: why are the elementary school students stressed and why are we fixing that stress with neo-liberal solutions rather than by changing the material conditions that cause that stress?), some parents were worried that to teach yoga would be to introduce non-Christian values into the school. In 2021, when Jeremy Gray introduced a bill to bring yoga instruction to k-12 schools in Alabama, he faced similar opposition, even as he and Ari

Shapiro agreed, when Shapiro interviewed him for NPR's *All Things Considered*, that neither Gray's Christianity nor Shapiro's Judaism had been threatened by their respective years of yoga practice.

For me, the interesting question is not whether yoga is Hindu, or infects a Christian or a Jew with Hinduism. I have no idea whether this is true, though I suspect that I think that the answer is "it depends on the example and on what you mean by 'Christian,' 'Jew,' and 'Hindu.'" Rather, I am interested in what American public schools have done when faced with these critiques. In response to these concerns, and in an attempt to make sure the yoga was not bringing in pernicious non-Christianity to the public schools, the school district did a number of things to make the yoga less Hindu, which included removing the word "namaste" from the curriculum. Now, to be honest, because of my discomfort with exoticism, I think this is just fine. The 2015 debate was, however, an opportunity for NPR reporter Deepak Singh to reflect on the word. Singh offers a literal translation of the word: "namaste" means "I bow before you." He talks about what it looks like in yoga classes in the US, hands before your heart, elbows parallel to the floor, eyes closed. Americans, who even pronounce the word differently than Indians, seem, he writes, to think of it as "a Hindu mantra, a divine chant, a yoga salutation," not what it means in India: hello or goodbye. Or, if you are trying to get rid of someone, something more like, "Good day to you, sir," in dismissal. Just as "goodbye" can mean all of those things in English, Singh talks about the many uses—including subversive—that he and his siblings found for the word "namaste." There is, he suggests, a formality to the word—it gets dragged out when you are performing for your parents' friends. He used it to get out of touching people's feet, normally the ultimate expression of respect. It was basically a negotiation—he was showing some respect, but not as much as he should have. His sister used the word to try to get their parents' friends, when she felt they were overstaying their welcome, to head home. Here, the word basically meant, "Don't let me keep you," or more candidly, "Don't let the door hit your ass on the way out."

The problem is not that the use of namaste in American yoga classes means something else. It is that this usage does not leave room for Singh's mouthy sister or for my Chachi, who always arrives saying "Namasteji, namasteji" in a way that is more like walking into a room saying "Ciao! Ciao!" and kissing people's cheeks than it is like a spiritual greeting.

But again, theoretically, it is not a problem if a word comes to have a new meaning when it migrates. In India, pajama was originally a word that simply meant the drawstring trousers that clothe the lower half of the body, for both men and women. It has its origins in Urdu and Persian. The British encountered pajamas when they colonized India, where they took what had been potentially formal wear and turned it into nightwear. You will notice that I am not railing against the use of the word pajamas.

The romanticization of namaste, however? That can have consequences.

Romanticization is erasure that looks like inclusion or appreciation. This is, I think, part of Lucia's point about exoticization, and it is, perhaps, most evident in Western responses to the word "namaste." Years ago, I was sitting in synagogue, listening to a lay High Holidays sermon. The speaker was talking about a trip he had taken to India some years before, and it sounded like a personally transformative experience and like every positive take on India by a Western tourist ever, when they are doing a positive spin—he talked about the colors and the smells. He did not talk about the poverty. He described trying to find the neighborhood with the old synagogues in it, and how helpful random people on the street were. Not, something he argued, you would see in the United States. That helpfulness. The willingness to go out of your way for another person was, he argued, connected to "namaste," the Hindi word for hello and goodbye, which he explained means, "that which is divine in me bows before that which is divine in you." I already knew this definition, in that you cannot have the hippie street cred that I have and *not* know it, but when he made the comment, as I sat in the choir loft in the back of our rented church, several thoughts popped into my head.

The point of his story was to talk about how good and generous and giving Indian people are, as compared to people in the US, to which I call bullshit. People in India are people, made of blood and bowel, just like the rest of us. What people in India often are is desperately poor, and I can believe that their helpfulness—going out of their way to act as a guide—could well have been done in hopes of a tip. Sure, they might have been acting out of the goodness of their hearts—just as, the month before I heard this story, I watched as an entire subway car of New Yorkers helped a mom with her two kids figure out how to find the hotel where she was meeting her husband. She and the kids had flown in from Minnesota to join him for a vacation on the tail end of his business trip, and she was on the wrong subway. It was midafternoon. The subway was not crowded. Not only did the entire car engage in a lively debate about the best way to fix her mistake (the bus, but buses are harder to navigate than trains), but someone got out at Union Station to point her in the right direction. This woman received help for a number of reasons. New Yorkers are both salt of the earth and really into giving directions (though they too are just people), and she was also helped by the fact that it was not rush hour, and let's not kid ourselves, by the fact that she was white and attractive. Still, I should note that I have been assaulted on public transit twice, and both times, men who were total strangers rescued me, pretending to know me, extricating me, and walking me to safety. You do not need a form of hello that acknowledges the divine in all to help others.

As I was listening to this man speak at shul, it struck me as weird that a man living in a massive suburban city could move through Mumbai without seeing or commenting on the children living in poverty, could come back talking about how Indian reverence for life is encoded in the very word for hello. It would be like looking at the wall slicing through Jerusalem and talking about how, because the word in Hebrew (and, come to think of it, in Arabic) for "Hello" translates to "Peace," Israel must be a peaceful place.

But as I noted, the speaker was talking about the helpfulness of the people who helped him search for synagogues—a helpfulness that he saw as born out of a worldview demonstrated by saying, every time you say hello, "That which is divine in me bows before that which is divine in you." The speaker's sermon mostly touched on the hospitality he and his wife had received at the Chabad House in Mumbai during their long-ago trip. Chabad is, essentially, a movement of very Orthodox Judaism that has a missionary bent—but missionary, Jewish style. Members of this movement are not interested in getting people who are not Jewish to become Jewish. They are interested in getting Jews to be more observant. They set up community centers all over the world—Chabad Houses—where they create warmth and community, hoping to teach people through example, to be more religiously observant Jews. But for the speaker, more recent events had altered his understanding of that idyllic visit.

The previous November, probably about ten or eleven months before I heard him speak, the Chabad House had been one of the sites of a four-day coordinated terror attack that rocked Mumbai. On November 26, 2008, terrorists had taken control of the Chabad House. Six people, including the couple that ran the house, were killed.

The man preaching was devastated. He had, understandably, felt particularly connected to these people whom he had met, who had offered him hospitality, based on their shared identity as Jews. (It is worth commenting that I had not been offered hospitality when I had visited an Indian Chabad House, and many members of the congregation—the interfaith couples, the queers, the converts, the Jewish kids who had Jewish fathers but not Jewish mothers—would not have been offered that same degree of hospitality either. Chabad tries to discourage interfaith marriage; rejects the Jewish identity of people whose fathers, but not mothers, are Jewish; and does not accept non-Orthodox conversions. While they might be pleasant to people who are not straight, they do not see queer relationships as in keeping with observant Jewish life. But that opinion is another way that this sermon was tone deaf and not really the point, at least not at the moment.) Of course, he was most upset about the murder of these people whom he had met. But at no point in the sermon did the speaker mention the more than 150 other people who died (not counting the nine attackers, who had, at the very least, decided to take a calculated risk, but who were also people). By and large, the people whose deaths were not mentioned in this High Holiday sermon were brown. They were the people who say "namaste," but for whom it simply means "hello" or "goodbye" and is not a theological statement.

I complained bitterly to the rabbi about the sermon, and now, no one can speak on a major holiday without having their remarks cleared ahead of time. The rabbi also talked to the speaker. Apparently, initially, he had planned to say something about all the dead and was horrified to realize that, in his editing and cutting to hit the time limit, he had neglected to deliver that line acknowledging them. The rabbi pointed out that I write a lot and could surely understand how this omission could happen.

I do, and I can. But I also want to suggest that where brown people *do* show up in this story matters. When someone frames you as so much nicer than the people back home, ties your extra niceness to a romanticized notion of your spirituality, motivations, and language; misses, romanticizes, or catastrophizes your material situation; and basically makes you part of the scenery, they have failed to create a story in which you are not scenery. Of course, this speaker edited out the actual Indians, the vast majority of the victims, the people whose culture and country he was visiting, and the people (if we mean the Indian Jews) whose culture Chabad is actively working to erase. He had seen them in a way that meant that they could not be the protagonists of his tale.

I have talked about this like I have answers, or like I do not appropriate. That as someone brown, as someone South Asian American, I am the subject of, the victim of appropriation, and not someone who ever falls into appropriation. Leaving aside the question of whether it is appropriation that my high school friends taught me to pull stuck toast out of the toaster with wooden chopsticks, or that Viet Thanh Nguyen changed my life forever when he tweeted about seeing someone eat Cheetos with chopsticks, I leave you with this example.

In 2016–2017, I spent the year in Washington, DC, at the Library of Congress. Sometimes, on my lunch break, I would walk over to Eastern Market, where, several days of the week, there is an actual market. One of the vendors was a woman from Nigeria who made and sold both traditional Nigerian clothing and skirts made out of Nigerian fabric and fabric from other parts of east Africa. The clothing was beautiful. She had an impressive set of extension cords that allowed her to sew in her booth, so I knew that she was the tailor. She charged reasonable prices for tailored clothing in the United States—the skirts were around $150 apiece. As someone with an abiding interest in textiles, I couldn't help but be fascinated. I have, in my day, quilted. I embroider and knit. I am a terrible dressmaker, but I know what good tailoring looks like, and this woman was good. I really wanted a skirt or two, but I did not want to inappropriately co-opt another culture.

I thought about it a lot. Many of the same questions I've mulled over in relation to Indian culture came to mind for me as I considered this woman and her wares. What counts as appropriation? Where are the lines between cultural exchange and appropriation best drawn? How do we honor and learn about other cultures, enjoying their beauty, without harming something or someone in the process of our own enjoyment? In the end, I decided to purchase some skirts. I was supporting a business owned by a Black woman. I was paying a good, fair rate for quality craftsmanship. I did not buy the traditional Nigerian outfits, but I did buy skirts made from the Nigerian fabric, skirts that were not notably different from what I might have made myself with a pattern from Simplicity or Butterrick, but were, perhaps, slightly different than a circle skirt.

I felt good about the purchase. I wore one of the skirts to class—once. A Nigerian student said that she loved that I had a Nigerian skirt. But that was the only time I wore it. After all was said and done, I did not feel comfortable wearing the skirts. I was not wearing the skirts like a costume—I was wearing them with the same long-sleeved black tops, black tights, and tall boots that I always wore; and they were just skirts, not something that required special skill to pin or wrap, but I was still worried about appropriation. I did not think my student's enthusiasm authorized my clothing choices. Today, years later, those beautiful skirts are languishing in my closet. I still feel good about the purchase—about supporting a Black woman-owned business—but I am not sure about wearing the clothing. And as those skirts sit in my closet, just as the saris sat in the closets of those white women at that long-ago Unitarian wedding, or, quite frankly, as my own saris do, I find myself wondering what the solution might be—where the lines are between competing values, and how we might find a line between appreciation and appropriation.

And here is the thing: the answer is hard, because it is contextual. As I have said, at least at this moment, I am not comfortable wearing my Nigerian skirts. But as my friend Kristie Soares, also known as the critical race scholar in the office next door, pointed out to me, it is fundamentally different for me to wear a Nigerian skirt than it was for the Unitarian ladies to attend a wedding in a sari. As Kristie reminded me, I am a person of color. Wearing ethnic clothing draws attention to myself, in a way that might well put me at risk in any number of settings. The white women wedding attenders took on no risk at all when they donned saris. In addition, India has never colonized Nigeria. Now, Indians have had complicated and not particularly pretty histories in Africa, and I cannot say for certain that each of those sari-wearing white ladies was of British decent (though the United States was not what you would call awesome to India during the Cold War). The racialized power dynamics and the histories of political power and influence are complicated, but however you parse them, I am very differently politically located. That said, both they and I are Americans, with all the economic and political power that such citizenship entails. To Kristie's responses, I would add that they bought their saris in India, where I presume they haggled, though they likely could have afforded to pay the asking price. I bought my skirts in Washington, DC, after saving up to pay the price, set to US prices for custom-made clothing. And I would note that I have the skill set required to wear a skirt, and the underwear. The young sari-wearers had neither of those things. So, maybe it is okay for me to wear the skirts. Certainly, it is more okay than it is for those white women to wear saris. But you know what? It is also perhaps less okay for me to wear those skirts than for my mom to wear a sari. And other than her skill, you cannot tell her apart from those white women. And I am not sure that my annoyance in yoga studios is fair. And so, the skirts collect dust, and when I move, I hunt for a pool and not a yoga studio, but still, I fish toast out of the toaster with wooden chopsticks and eat popcorn with metal ones that can go in the dishwasher. The fact that I do not know does not mean that I cannot be wrong. It just means that the answers are neither easy, nor obvious.

Six

MENTORING

My educational experiences left me with a near-total absence of South Asians, people who looked like me, in my academic training, or of East Asians or Asian Americans who did not look like me. Every teacher I had in my K–12 education was white, and while I can think of one or two Asian faculty members at my undergraduate institution, while I was there, none of them were tenure track in the areas that I studied. I was in grad school before I saw my first South Asian woman on the faculty. I was in my first tenure-track position before I had my first South Asian mentor. She was also a visiting faculty member, though there were other South Asian women employed by that university—but they were not humanists and worked on the other side of campus. I am not sure I ever had coffee with them.

I have thought quite a bit about how to write about that experience, and about what to say. I have thought about writing an op-ed, with observations and recommendations, but in the end, I am not someone who studies education, or educational psychology. I am simply someone who has a lot of thoughts about what it means to know that Marian Wright Edelman had a real point when she said, "You can't be what you can't see," but who also managed, despite the lack of precise role models, to pull off a career—and to do so with amazing mentorship from a wide range of people. Still, despite the amazing mentors I have had, I find myself with something to say: mentors who look like you matter, as do communities of people who look like you, but also, and perhaps more importantly, so are mentors and communities of people who share some of your experiences. And that probably means that you need a network.

In my own life, I have a network, and it has been rich and in many ways, it has been wonderful, but it has often lacked people who are like me. And so, I have to acknowledge from the outset that I am writing about something I imagine—what it would be like to have a mentor who was, like me, a US-born mixed person with a South Asian parent.

I can remember a visiting South Asian professor at my undergraduate alma mater. I never studied with her. I remember her, though, because she made me tea in her kitchen, and we talked. When I met her fifteen years later, at a conference, she remembered my name. I have not seen her again, though I could reach out, and I have wondered: was it rare for her to see a student that looked like her? Does she realize that I remember her, giving me tea and drinking water out of a metal tumbler like the ones in my parents' home?

I remember one tenure-track male Asian faculty member from my master's program. Whether there really was only one, or whether I am forgetting someone, or did not notice someone—that is harder to say. In my PhD program, I encountered an Asian professor, here or there, a tenure-track or visiting faculty member, but I do not remember them teaching doctoral seminars. I certainly never studied with them. By then, I had learned not to look for Asians. I assumed I would not find them, and I did not yet know I needed them. And they were not studying in the fields that interested me. People assumed that I must be interested in Hinduism studies or South Asian studies, rather than American religion.

Two thoughts on this experience—and maybe three: I think it's important to note that at each of my educational institutions, there was a Black professor who stepped up and into that mentoring role for me, and each of these people meant the world to me. They mentored me through intellectual and academic challenges. They were present when I encountered racism or sexism in the classroom. They tried to work from their positionality, to help me with mine. When I think about how many students of color knock on my own door today, I marvel that these professors found the time.

In my first position as a professional, a "pre-doc" one-year position at a small liberal arts college, I was assigned a professional mentor, a Latina English professor and poet. She was the first person to talk to me about how to read faculty meetings and inserted some cynicism into my experience of the academy—she was the first person to flat out tell me that no matter how well I played the game, it was never going to make up for the systemic oppression that structures the idealistic and high-minded ivory tower just as much as any other profession. I was not ready to hear that message. I was still dangerously invested in the model minority myth that had consistently worked for me, and she did not judge (at least not too hard) and was there (and did not say "I told you so") when years later, I came to her incandescent with rage at racism and sexism. But she also taught me other skills that I needed help with—how to wear makeup in the academy and what brand of makeup was best for the intersection of "person of color" and "concerned about animal cruelty."

But these mentors, as much love and gratitude as I feel toward them, were still not people who shared either of my key experiences—my experience as an Asian American or my experience of mixedness.

This separation from my own experience was, of course, actually true of the Asian mentors that I encountered as well, certainly the South Asian mentors. Asian immigration to the United States was tightly restricted from the 1920s until 1965, and there wasn't a huge amount of South Asian immigration (though there was some) before the 1920s. The first census to count South Asians, in 1910, recorded just over 2,500 "Hindus," despite the fact that many of those early immigrants were Panjabi Sikhs. It wasn't until 1980 that South Asian immigration to the United States really took off. According to the South Asian Digital Archive, between 1980 and 2013, the "Indian immigrant population" doubled every decade, going from 206,000 to 2.04 million.

What this means, for me, as a mixed race South Asian American, is that the majority of my South Asian mentors or colleagues are immigrants. It is only in my generation, or in people slightly older, that we begin to see plenty of Asian Americans moving through society—people who could be our teachers, doctors, therapists, vice presidents. (My therapist, who I've seen for the last several years, is half–South Asian and half-white, and at least a decade older than me. She is an anomaly, and I am lucky to have found someone who shares so many of my racial and cultural contexts.) And while "people who look like me" are important, Asian mentors, even immigrants who have learned a huge amount about their adopted country, are working against a culture gap. (Worried that I was being unfair to immigrants, I asked a friend of mine who moved to the United States from South Korea at twenty-four whether she feels a culture gap with her children. She laughed at me for even needing to ask.)

My South Asian mentors have a very different relationship to their home country than I have. Of course, what that relationship actually is varies greatly from person to person. Are you homesick? Or are you critical of the place that you left and glad to be here? Do you like American culture, by and large, or does it seem endlessly strange and/or less than the culture you left? Did you come here by choice or necessity? Always, there are variations and differences. Some of us who were born here never go to South Asia. Some of us make the journey every year. But few of us have spent lots of time in school there. Sometimes we are strangers in a strange land; sometimes it is almost home.

This kind of South Asian mentor, few and far between though they were, often had the additional status of being immigrants. They were not Indian American. But it is also true that for many of us growing up in the 1970s, 1980s, and 1990s, mentors who immigrated as adults had different class positions than those of us who grew up the children of early immigrants. This distinction shapes all sorts of things, but largely it creates misunderstandings. Sometimes those misunderstandings are about culture. Other times they are about class.

My South Asian mentors or immigrant colleagues often misunderstand some fundamental aspects of American life, or at least have very different takes on it from those of us who grew up here. Often, and here I am speaking as someone in the humanities, my colleagues who make their way to the United States come from positions of notable economic privilege. Thanks to deep familial financial investment, they could relocate to the US without needing to go into medicine or business to send money home. Of course, not every immigrant comes from that kind of luxury (and of course, many American academics *also* come from luxury), but what I mean here is that the gap between someone steeped in that economic background and someone who grew up as a working-class American may be wider than one might think based solely on ethnicity.

There is a culture gap between Asian Americans who came from struggling immigrant families with no inherited wealth, and less capital than they would have enjoyed if they had not been sending money to the family back home, and some of the elite intellectuals who immigrate into the American academic world or come to the United States to practice medicine or work in lucrative tech fields. It also means that sometimes, unless you are a person of particular sensitivity, you miss certain things. While obviously there are children of immigrants who come from very wealthy families (a friend whose father is a doctor with an elite medical specialty once said to me, "You can say it. My father is part of the 1 percent"), many of us children of immigrants have a much more middle-class existence. Put differently, because of the restrictions governing that early era of immigration, many of us today are children of the professional class but without inherited wealth and with obligations to family back home. We, the children of those immigrants, left school with the student loans that are so much in the news as a defining characteristic of Generation Xers and millennials. We struggle to gather down payments on homes, for example, especially when, as people of color, we are often more comfortable in cities—which are notoriously more expensive than many rural areas.

Not only is inherited family money often lacking, but these households often have less disposable income or savings than their annual incomes might suggest, as well. Right from the start, long before saving or investing, the immigrant generation was sending money home or launching relatives on their own paths to immigration. (I might be telling the story of my own family here, but I know it is shared by others.) We grew up living with modest means. We went to public schools. For some families, this meant vacations were trips back to India or the great American road trip—with Best Westerns or sleeping bags in the basements of other Indian families. My own version of this story involves road trips to my American grandparents in Illinois, my dad's cousins in Montreal, or my parents' closest college friends in Vermont, DC, and Ontario. We drove from New Haven to see sand dunes in Michigan and to DC for the free museums, or toured the Ben and Jerry's factory in Vermont. The fanciest accommodations we ever had were roadside motels with pools (instead of roadside motels without pools). My experience is the experience of the American working or middle class. We could not afford the occasional visit to India.

I once sat and listened to a group of Asian and Asian Americans talking about the college admissions process in the United States—specifically the college visit. Some of the Asians were marveling at the phenomenon of the "college visit," the idea that American parents will take their high school students to see prospective colleges. To them, it seemed like an amazing luxury. It was decadent. It was privilege writ large. It was a sign of American entitlement. One of the other women in the conversation was, like me, an ABCD. Later she and I talked about this discussion, and we were steamed. We had both gone on those college-visit trips. They had been the family drives—like any other road trip, but with colleges rather than historic sites as the destination. My friend and I had slept in dorms. Our respective parents had stayed with friends. It was galling to have someone with servants in the family home complain about the luxury of this tradition—someone who had been able to go to college without student loans! And yet, it was hard to push back without looking like an entitled American.

I have listened to people who went to private schools in Pakistan or India and then had enough money to come to the United States for college, paying full tuition in US dollars, talk about the blinding privilege of the students at (granted) high-end universities when at least 10 percent of the campus is food insecure. I have heard people who live off the same salary as I do, but with no student loans to pay, talk about the decadence of American life. Honestly, it is also, perhaps, easier to go for ideological purity over pragmatism when you are not saddled with student loans or worried, actively, about caring for aging parents at US prices. And of course, our class backgrounds shape all sorts of things—our pragmatism versus our idealism, our ability to critique the "home" cultures, the power that we do or do not have to innovate, and so forth. Once again, there is a similar class spread among people who are born in the United States, and not all South Asian immigrants come from the upper crust, but more than once I and another American-born South Asian from that first wave of immigration, particularly those of us in the academy, have been struck by how massive a class gap there is between our experiences and the experiences of many of our immigrant colleagues. It requires an immense act of imagination and empathy for those immigrants to understand that some of the apparent comforts of American life are disguising some large differences.

So, all of this is to say that when the mentors are Asian, there is a range of cultural (and often class) gaps to take into account. That doesn't mean that they cannot be good mentors. That first South Asian mentor of mine is a woman of empathy, who approaches other people's lives with openness, rather than judgment. But this requires a kind of imagination that not all people, or even most people, have. And even the rare South Asian, or South Asian American, mentor is lacking the experience that is central to my experience, as someone with one South Asian parent: the experience of blended heritage.

Why is a mentor with an experience of mixedness important? Mostly, because being mixed is a distinct experience. For instance, I have often been in mentoring spaces for people of color where people have talked about the white people who have let them down—failures of allyship or friends who turned out not to be allies when the chips are down. These are important conversations—they are necessary and vital conversations. But often, not always, but often, they veer into conversations about how you cannot trust white people, any white people. Now, sometimes, to be sure, these people are also in mixed race romantic relationships, so it is not like they cannot be in conversations or relationships with white people. But if you object, then you are demonstrating white fragility or denying the reality that not all white parents do due diligence in raising non-white children.

(And I am going to take a moment to suggest that a hard reality may be that there is no such thing as enough due diligence for white parents doing the work of parenting interracial kids in a racist society—all the theoretical knowledge in the world, and all the best intentions may not be enough to fill in the gaps caused by their positionality. Which does not mean that it cannot be done well, or that it should not be attempted, just that part of the deal with parenting—I say as a non-parent—seems to be that people fail in any number of ways despite their best intentions and attempts. This is just one more way.)

But in the context of mentoring or of affinity groups, what does it do to the mixed race person with a white parent to tell them no white people can be trusted? What does it do if that person is an adolescent? What does it do to their ability to share their networks and sources of support? More importantly, since white parents will probably inevitability fail their children of color as those children learn to navigate the realities of race in American culture, or as the white parents fail to notice their own racial biases—but also given that we love, trust, and need our parents—people who present the foolhardiness of ever trusting white people are not providing space for those of us who have close kin among the oppressing group. They are not giving us space to do the hard work of learning how to clearly see the failures of our parents, so that we can navigate them, negotiate them, and learn to be people of color in an oppressive society, while also having the warm and loving relationships that we want with our parents.

Of course, there are differences in mixed experiences—in how you are read, racially, in the world, in how your individual parents decided to navigate their interracial, intercultural relationship. Where and how you are raised also matters. For instance, my friend Jimmy talks about how he was raised on army bases where all the Korean people he knew, growing up, were Korean women married to Black or white GIs, or their children. To have one Korean and one American parent was what it was to be Korean and therefore he did not have the same anxieties about authenticity that I had, growing up on the edge of an immigrant community where my mother's white Americanness, and the American aspects of our home, made us somewhat suspect. Even when Jimmy got to college and saw LA's Koreatown, which he loved and identified as primarily for people who were differently Korean than he was, he did not feel like his way of being Korean was inauthentic.

He also does not identify as mixed, for reasons that are both intellectual/theoretical and personal. (He also heard and did not argue with me when I explained that I do.) Clearly in some ways, Jimmy's needs might have been different than mine, in part because of where he grew up, in part because of the communities available to him. I do not mean to suggest a monolithic mixed experience. But at the same time, while we may relate differently to experiences of boundary crossing and code switching, to questions of authenticity or of multiple senses of belonging, they are experiences about which we can have a particular kind of conversation. Spaces for those conversations are important. And so, this is not only an argument for the importance of mentors who share that experience of multiple heritages, but for communities of people who do.

Just like there is no single Indian American (or Korean American or Mexican American) experience, there is no universal experience for people that the US census refers to as people of "two or more races." But there are aspects of that conversation that are, perhaps, unique to those experiences. A friend (and mentor) of mine who is Italian and Mexican American floated the idea that being mixed necessitates a flexibility of thinking that both is intrinsically valuable and, sometimes, to others, appears wishy-washy. While you are seeing many points of view, others can hear you saying, "There are fine people on both sides." But it is not that the mixed person does not see, for instance, their white relatives participating in systemic oppression. It is just that we have to learn to separate out the individual, and his or her feelings and points of view—blind spots included—from the systems that they enact. Sometimes, that tendency probably is wishy-washy. Other times, it is certainly damaging to us. But perhaps, sometimes, the skills and mental flexibility of blended heritages also offer a way forward.

One argument is that it is not the job of, in my case, Asian people to teach me how to be mixed race, or how to navigate racism, including the white privilege and fragility of my own white relatives, while having important family relationships with those white people, but the reality is that I have not had very many opportunities to have mixed mentors. For those of us who are Asian and white and in Generation X (or who are older millennials), there weren't many mixed mentors to look to. And so, we had to choose between white spaces or non-white spaces, and in some ways, since neither of those spaces were meant for us, in the end, they both fail us.

I do not mean to say that people of color do not deserve spaces where they can be as angry at white people as they need and want to be and perhaps specifically at white people who have betrayed their trust. It is just that those moments, at least for this mixed race person, need more nuance. And they are moments that tend to silence the mixed race person who is struggling to navigate the failures of their white loved ones. If I accept the premise that white people are fundamentally not to be trusted, what does that do to my relationship to the white woman who grew me in her body, who nursed me for two years, picked gravel out of my knees, washed my hair in the kitchen sink, read me children's books before bed and (in adulthood) after bad breakups, took out a second mortgage to send me to college, came to take me to get surgery when I was thirty-eight, canceled work to be with me when I had to put down a dog when I was forty, read over this entire manuscript and described it as "hard to read in places, but fair." And who has let me down, even as she tried hard and supported me in major ways, around issues of race. And who was learning and doing her best to be the white mother of brown daughters on the fly without the role models or mentors that, in the end, we all need.

Mixed race people need space for talking about those experiences. They need, when possible, mentors who share their experience of mixedness. They need spaces that are for people who share their ethnic heritage, but also spaces to talk about what it means to have blended heritage. Those of us whose mixture includes white family need spaces to explore our relationship to whiteness—both the places where it has given us advantages to have white family and places where it has hurt us. We need to have space where it is not seen as failing to love yourself because you continue to care for your racist grandmother, or cousin, or half-sibling.

A mentor of mine, a woman who has a white parent and a Black parent, hears my shame at talking to Black friends about microaggressions, or my surprise when the racism in my life is not micro, and suggests that part of my difficulties is tied to being mixed. To be mixed, she suggests, means to have half of your family not really understand the world that you are navigating, as compared to people who have families that talked about racism, and that made sure that their family members had messages that specifically combatted the racism that they faced. Whereas I grew up in a family in which microaggressions were not well articulated or understood. I do not mean to suggest that microaggressions and macroaggressions, like police brutality, are the same thing, but I do want to suggest that those of us with interracial families in which many relatives are white, need mentors who can help us navigate the microaggressions that come from within our families. We need spaces that allow for that reality, and people who will help us learn from and navigate those challenges. They are challenges that exist outside of our families as well. One should absolutely be able to call out, and perhaps even cancel the "Karens" of our lives, but what do you do when the Karen that you are canceling at work or in the neighborhood exhibits behavior that you see in your family?

It is not, perhaps, the responsibility of Asian Americans to provide spaces for those conversations, but for people of my generation, other mixed people—particularly if you want them to be your particular mix—are few and far between. And to have spaces where a distrust of white people is part of the currency can put someone squarely in between the politics of the group and their love and loyalty to their white relatives, which can, in turn, make it harder to process the moments when their white relatives have failed them. Authenticity apart from, as well as our loyalty to, love for, and trust in, our families can make us feel out of place in (certain) POC spaces, or our sense of nuance can feel like apologetics to them. I am not sure that they are wrong, but I am not sure that I am either.

Seven

THE RACISM OF PEOPLE
WHO LOVE YOU

I was sitting in a restaurant with my friend, one of my dearest friends, a white friend, a male friend, a gay friend, but gay in an upper-middle-class white kind of way that comes with kinds of privilege not normally associated with the word queer.

I don't remember why we were talking about racism, but something prompted me to say, "there is a lot of racism out there, and all of it sucks, but the kind that really hurts me is the casual racism of people who love me."

James looked stricken, as if I had hit him, and asked me, "Are you talking about me?" And then, all of a sudden, I did not know what to say. I hadn't meant to be talking about him. I was talking in generalities, about something that happens more than I would like, as a person of mixed race, with both white family members and a predominantly white professional and social world. And so I had not been fishing, but at the same time, I realized that I had also been talking about him.

One of the hardest challenges for me, in living among and deeply loving white people, is the question of how to talk to them about their own racism, when it comes up, either in reference to me or in their interactions with the world. When I experience racism from the people whom I love most and, perhaps more importantly, from people who love me, I am always surprised, taken aback, and disappointed.

When someone does what James did, in that moment, and asks if they have hurt me with their racism, I am always flustered, because, if you are a person of color in a conversation with a white person, there is risk involved in answering the question, especially if the answer is yes.

The risk is this: if you say yes, "you are the person I am talking about. You have done racist things and you have hurt me," you risk losing your friend—they may be hurt and angry that you could say such a thing.

Or they may deny that what they did was racist—if you were hurt, it is because you are too sensitive. That is, of course, another way of losing your friend.

And if you say, "No, I am not talking about you," if you lie, then you lose them, just in a different way.

That risk is intensified if the person in question is someone whom you love, and who loves you, be it a friend, a partner, a family member—risking the loss of love is terrifying.

But if these realities are hard when they come up in conversation, they are so much harder in the moment when the racism is actually occurring. James asked if I was talking about him—if his own racism had hurt me. Part of why I was afraid to say yes was because, on the day I was remembering, I had called him a racist, and we had almost lost each other.

Maybe ten years before our conversation, I was visiting James. He was living abroad for work, and so the visit was a long one—two carefully carved-out weeks, with an airline flight on the way. As I was heading out of the Atlanta airport, I had what

I tend to describe as a "TSA run-in." Now, years later, I actually do not remember what this particular incident included. In the days before the full-body scans, I was routinely pulled aside for extra pat downs, sometimes in private rooms, far more intrusive than you might realize if you have never been subjected to one. Occasionally, I would stand by my bag, as every carefully folded item was unfolded and examined, leaving me running late, with a pile of rumpled clothing. Probably this was one of those times. But whatever had happened, it had been both frightening and embarrassing. And, relatively early on in my visit, my experience came up.

James commented that I had to remember that they were scanning people based on trends and demographics. If I met some of the TSA criteria, which I did, because I am brown and have a Muslim first name, and therefore came under extra scrutiny, and that extra scrutiny kept everyone, including me, safer, then so be it. My response was to talk about what that experience felt like, and what other TSA experiences had felt like—I told him that it was degrading, humiliating, and scary.

He argued for the system, basically saying that a big system, like the TSA, could not make their decisions based on whether individuals disliked being searched—it was not reasonable to expect them to take feelings into account. He kept returning to the point that being searched made everyone safer, including me. And if the cost of that safety was some small inconvenience, so be it.

When I said that it was not a small inconvenience, he asked how long the delay was and whether I had ever missed a flight. I haven't, but certainly I have found myself getting on airplanes having seen my mealtime evaporate. I now have anxiety about flying, not about the actual flight, but about what humiliating and frightening things might happen in the security line.

But really, the point was that the extra searches are dehumanizing. If they occur in public, you are then labeled as different, as other, in front of everyone else in the line. Your bags are opened, your underwear, medications, and any other private items are lifted out of your bags and displayed, however unintentionally, to your fellow passengers. If the search is in private, you are asked to remove most of your clothing and you are touched, by a gloved stranger, more intimately that you are touched by most doctors.

For me, all of these encounters come with an overlay of fear. I am a woman. I am brown. And for most of my life, I have been financially strapped. Not the grinding poverty that traps entire communities, but I grew up in a household that often sent any extra money back to relatives in India. As an adult, I have always been student broke, where the resources that I had were rarely sufficient to deal with unexpected financial bumps in the road and where any of those bumps could wipe out my disposable income for months.

I am aware, as well, that the systemic racism that led to me being pulled out of a line could, at any moment, turn into vitriolic, personal racism or could become dangerous, while staying impersonal and systemic. And so, whenever these airport encounters happen, I move through them desperately trying to repress the fight-or-flight response that I worry would make me look flighty or dangerous.

I tried to explain all of this to James, but I was upset and not terribly articulate. I tried to present him with the range of my experience, but his response was to tell me to argue with logic rather than with emotions. That he would not listen to arguments based in emotions. As a response, what he said felt sexist. But it also made me feel very much that my friend, one of the people I loved most in the world and someone whose love I have always taken for granted, did not care that any time I flew, I ran the risk of a terrifying and dehumanizing experience. Far more than our disagreement, his discounting of the emotional weight of my experience hurt me.

I reacted in anger, and I told him that when he announced that he did not care about my experience as a person of color, he was being racist. That fundamentally, it was only through emotions that I could convey that experience, and if he thought that the emotions of people of color did not matter, well, then he was racist.

Stung by what I had said, he stalked off and went to bed. I sat on his living room couch, crying and trying to figure out how to change my flight so that I could go home early. I was crying because, whether or not he had meant to, my friend had just implicitly told me that, because I am brown, I did not deserve to be treated with dignity. I was crying because, in his refusal to hear and listen to what it is like to walk in my skin, something had broken in me. And I could not imagine how I could accept his hospitality for another week and a half.

Sick with emotion and sadness, both about my friend's words and about our argument, I knocked on his bedroom door. He was lying on his stomach, looking at his computer. "We'll talk about it tomorrow," he said.

The next night, we met for dinner. We returned to the previous night's conversation and he said, "So, you think I am racist." And looking at him, I was unwilling to deny that essentially, I did. I remember him looking away from me, staring across the table, over my left shoulder. "That's great, Samira. That's just great."

He was furious, largely, I think, because he was hurt. As the writer, speaker, and sociologist Allan G. Johnson has written, very few white people, especially good, earnest, justice-focused white people, want to see themselves as sources of racism. And, as he points out, this problem goes even further. "Given the strange but prevalent idea that we are what we do," Johnson writes, there is "a sort of one-drop rule by which a single racist act is all it takes to reveal ourselves as racist human beings."

In this formulation, if you do a racist thing, a single racist thing, you are bad person. Rhetorically, if one racist act makes someone a racist, the difference collapses between my deeply well-intentioned friend and someone who showed up in New Orleans to protest Ruby Bridges attending first grade, who beat Rodney King, who marched in Charlottesville with a torch to protest the removal of the statue of Robert E. Lee, who yelled at a school board meeting that teaching about race in American history is destroying the nation. And so, someone like my friend needs to reject the idea that he might have a perspective that is shaped by his whiteness and that supports systemic racism because he needs (and deserves) the distance between himself and the racism that he knows how to see.

I knew all this, but I was still furious. He had refused to act like my experience of racial profiling mattered and hadn't even told me that he was sorry that the precautions he considered necessary were so upsetting, but he felt entitled to make me out to be a bad person for calling him racist. And I could not imagine the next week and a half of living in his house.

But still, I was afraid of losing a dear friend if I changed my flights. And so, I backpedaled. In the end, I apologized, told him that I had been angry and that I shouldn't have said such things to him. I also, finally, came up with a logical argument against the racial profiling of the TSA. I said, "but we have, as a society, accepted that cops should not racially profile US citizens and that when they do (which they do all the time), it is harassment." "See," he said, "that is an argument that works for me. Give me logic. Don't give me your emotions."

For years, I chewed over this experience in my head. I remained angry, with him and with myself. With him for not acknowledging the validity of my affective response, but also for two other things.

In a 2017 study, the American Civil Liberties Union found that, despite the fact that the TSA claims not to profile based on ethnicity, race, or religion, they focus their screening on Arabs, Muslims, and Latinos. Furthermore, TSA's screening processes are so poorly grounded in research that, in 2013, the Government Accountability Office suggested limiting funding for some of their programs until their approaches could be scientifically demonstrated to keep people safe.

Granted, I did not know that at the time—I learned it later, because I had been ruminating on the experience. So James's logical argument was built, in the end, not on provable fact, but on a desire to feel safe, just as my affective argument had been.

His turn to logic was about the desire of a white person to feel safe. My friend does not have a lot of experience feeling unsafe. He is white, male, upper middle class, and though he is gay, most of the world reads him as straight—he can walk down the street with the total anonymity of the dominant group, even if he only partially belongs to it. He does not really know, in his bones, the insecurity that can come with femaleness or with brownness, just as I do not live with the uncertainty that I know comes with Blackness. And so, when James imagined TSA screenings, he assumed inconvenience, but not anxiety or real danger. It wasn't so much that he didn't care that his sense of safety required the sacrifice of mine, it was that he could not see that his sense of safety required the sacrifice of mine.

To him, the additional screening seemed like an inconvenience, but he could not and did not see that the screening struck me as almost as frightening as whatever terror attack it was meant to stave off. To him, as a white person, the police and security are there to ensure his safety, and, he assumes, mine. He presumes their good intentions, not only in their interactions with him, but in their interactions with me.

Logic, of course, is a trait traditionally associated with men, while emotion has always been framed as the realm of women. Emotion, then, counts less not because it is less important than logic, but because it is "female" and therefore less valuable. Just as those of us who are not white are also seen as being less logical, more in thrall of our emotions or our instincts. My friend was not intending to use sexist logic in his argument, any more than he had intended racism. He was simply operating from within his cultural norms—just as he had on the subject of race.

But the thing was that his call for logic was also a bit of a red herring. He was valuing his own safety and not seeing the ways in which his own safety was created, a set of priorities that are also born out of emotion—specifically out of fear.

It is blind spots like these that make racism so challenging. They are the blind spots of what Ta-Nehisi Coates calls "the good, racist people." In a *New York Times* essay of that name, he wrote, "In modern America we believe racism to be the property of the uniquely villainous and morally deformed, the ideology of trolls, gorgons and orcs." As Coates points out in his essay, which tells of the day that the famous actor Forest Whitaker had been stopped and frisked by an employee in Coates's neighborhood deli, for the crime of shopping while Black, though, that understanding of who is racist is not quite right.

The owner of the deli apologized, and, Coates says, seemed "sincerely mortified." The deli is very good. The people involved mean well, are sorry, are good people. In his essay, Coates clearly struggles with the question of whether to forgive them and return his patronage to the deli. In the end, he decides not to—he could not, he realizes, have been so understanding about their intentions if the accused Black man had been his own son. And besides, however good and convenient this particular deli is, there are other good and delicious delis in Manhattan, in the Upper West Side.

The problem that Coates is talking about, the racism of good people, is very much the problem that I am talking about, but in the end, while boycotting the deli works well, walking out on loved ones who have implicit bias or are shaped, as we all are, by racist assumptions, does not work for me.

What do you do about the people whom you cannot (or very much do not want to) remove from your life?

James taught me how to drive a manual-transmission car. When he was in the Peace Corps, he got a letter from my roommate, telling him that my boyfriend of years had left me, and he biked fifteen miles to a telephone that he could use to call me, just to listen to me cry and to tell me he loved me. Out of all my non-academic friends, James is one of only two who has loved me enough to learn about my world and to stand by me through years on the job market, when my sense of self was almost torn apart by my failing career. He drove me to my father's funeral.

What do you do when the good person who makes a mistake rooted in systemic oppression is a relative or your significant other or a friend whom you have loved for more than half your life? How do you make the decision when you can't simply find another deli?

Of course, some people of color have decided to incur lost friendships if it's the price of confronting racism. But when we speak of racist friends, we're not all discussing the same thing.

I understand why people walk out on friendships when they discover that a friend actually dislikes Black or brown people and demonstrates that racism through comments or behavior. But those examples are not the racism of good white people. It is not the structural racism that seeps into the assumptions and worldviews of people who mean well, and maybe even actively participate in anti-racist activities, but are also shaped by the world in which they live.

In the end, my friend and I had a hard conversation that night in the restaurant in 2016. As we sat there in the dim light and discomfort, I stirred my cocktail until the ice chipped and melted away and he shredded the garnish on the appetizer plate as we talked. But it wasn't an angry conversation, like the one we had almost a decade before. And when I told him that I had been considering writing this essay, he asked for anonymity, but he also told me to do it. And maybe that is what is important. While this is not a story of redemption—no one has overcome his or her positions in the world—here he is, trying this time, to listen across difference.

ACKNOWLEDGMENTS

My editor at Beacon, Amy Miller Caldwell, was a mentor before she was an editor. She has helped me develop this (and other) projects over the years, has taught me the ropes, and has pushed me to do more than I thought I could. When we started this project, we talked quite a bit about the ways that white people, with the best of intentions, end up letting down people of color, and she reminded me that she is a white editor. I would like to thank her for reading my stories and never flinching, and for helping me to articulate truths that she could not possibly have always found comfortable. My thanks to her, and to everyone at Beacon, especially Carol Chu, who designed the amazing cover, for bringing this book from an idea to something that could be on a bookstore shelf.

Over the years, many people have been conversation partners. I would particularly like to thank Brantley Bryant, Melissa Borja, M. Soledad Caballero, Jeremy Calder, Jung Choi, Allia Dhody, Anna Dhody, Sarah Imhoff, Khyati Y. Joshi, Harishita Mruthinti Kamanth, Shobhana Kanal, Isabel Koester, Sailajah Krishnamurti, Shreena Gandhi, Kathleen Holscher, Chrissy Lau, Sandra Lawson, Laura Arnold Leibman, Joshua Lesser, Laura Levitt, Jimmy McCarty, Linda Mehta, Deepti Misri, Celeste Montoya, Geeta Palshikar, Shreeyash Palshikar, Kwame Phillips, Claire Sufrin, Nishant Upadhyay, Judith

Weisenfeld, Alexis Wells-Oghoghomeh, Tisa Wenger, Candace West, and Debbie Whitehead for any number of conversations about race and identity over the years. Ben Brazil, Jack Downey, Adrienne Krone, Rachel Lindsay, Cameron McGlothlin, Cathy Muller, Melanie Monteclare Pace, Anthony Petro, Tom Smith, Kristie Soares, and in particular, Briallen Hopper, have both had those conversations and read and thoughtfully commented on drafts. Each of these readers has offered not only their insights, but pep talks at key moments, as has my writing accountability partner, Heather White. Tisa Wenger helped me work through final edits, and Ben Brazil offered a lakeside spot in which to make those edits. Stacia Pelletier has passed her keen editorial eye over every essay, and in doing so has helped me clarify my voice, and I am grateful.

I am someone who lives in and needs community. The first drafts of almost all of these essays were written in my very favorite coffee shop and bookstore: Uncle Bobbie's. I have missed your space every day since I moved away. I am grateful to the intellectual communities of my workplaces, first at Albright College and then in the Women and Gender Studies Department and the Program in Jewish Studies at the University of Colorado Boulder. At and beyond those institutions, I have been blessed with a rich intellectual community that is also a community of care. Many, but not all, members of that community are named above; I hope that its members know who they are and how much they matter to me. My writing groups, my Young Scholars of American Religion cohort, and my American Religious History Feminist Reading Group have been central to my intellectual, and also my emotional, life. Thank you also to the pillars of my family life, both family of blood and of choice: Fran, Calvin, Sam, Adrienne, Anthony, Ben and the rest of the Brazils, Cameron, Andrea, Matteo, Candace, Chris,

Eli, Liz, Charlie, Tova, Heather, Jenny, Jung, Kate, the Lauras, Melissa, Rachel, the Sarahs, Susannah, Josh, Tisa, Tom, Yoshimi, and, of course, Mommy z"l and Daddy z"l. Last, but not least, to Greta z"l, Maggie z"l, Quincy, and Daisy.

People from my life appear in these pages. I am particularly grateful to my mother, who has allowed me to tell less than comfortable stories, and to the friend who appears in these pages as James. He is not at his best in the story that I tell, but he was the strongest champion of the idea that I should write this book. I am grateful to him for letting me tell the story of one of our most painful fights in order to shine light on what unconscious and unintentional racism looks like in relationships of love.